THE **edge**
OF THE
centre

Mary Trainer

THE edge
OF THE
centre

celebrating naramata centre

WoodLake

Editor: Ingrid Turnbull
Cover and interior design: Verena Velten
Proofreader: Dianne Greenslade

 WoodLake is an imprint of Wood Lake Publishing, Inc. Wood Lake
Publishing acknowledges the financial support of the Government
of Canada, through the Book Publishing Industry Development
Program (BPIDP) for its publishing activities. Wood Lake Publishing also acknowledges the
financial support of the Province of British Columbia through the Book Publishing Tax Credit.

At Wood Lake Publishing, we practise what we publish, being guided by a concern for fairness,
justice, and equal opportunity in all of our relationships with employees and customers. Wood
Lake Publishing is an employee-owned company, committed to caring for the environment and
all creation. Wood Lake Publishing recycles, reuses, and encourages readers to do the same.
Resources are printed on 100% post-consumer recycled paper and more environmentally
friendly groundwood papers (newsprint), whenever possible. A percentage of all profit is
donated to charitable organizations.

Library and Archives Canada Cataloguing in Publication
Trainer, Mary, 1948-
    The edge of the centre : celebrating Naramata Centre / Mary Trainer.
ISBN 978-1-55145-574-7
    1. Naramata Centre--History. I. Title.
BV5068.R4T73 2009   267'.13097115   C2009-902004-1

Published by WoodLake
An imprint of Wood Lake Publishing Inc.
9590 Jim Bailey Road, Kelowna, BC, Canada, V4V 1R2
www.woodlakebooks.com
250.766.2778

Printing 10 9 8 7 6 5 4 3 2 1
Printed in Canada by
Houghton Boston, Saskatoon, SK

Dedication

To my mother, Dorothy Anna Morgan, former long-time resident of Summerland, B.C., who inspired me to explore, appreciate, and celebrate history.

and

To everyone who so enthusiastically and generously shared with me their stories and passion for Naramata Centre.

Table of Contents

Invitation

Welcome to *The Edge of the Centre.*

I invite you into this collection of remembrances of the past 60 years. I invite you to celebrate and affirm; question and wonder; understand and appreciate; and move into the next 60 years with the centre.

Naramata Centre is a place with a mission. It is a place of people called by God for a purpose. It is a layered and textured place, and one of many stories. Stories of the land and the lake. Stories of the centre as a place of retreat and learning. Stories of the people who come and go. Stories of those who come and stay. Stories of how the on-going call of God has led the centre to its unique programs, principles, and hospitality.

Allison Rennie

This book gives glimpses of the who and how and why of Naramata Centre. Imagine yourself there in the Winter Session of 1950, or on the board of 1963, or in the Senior Teen program in 2008. How will this experience continue to shape who we are as a centre beyond the edge of this moment? Imagine!

Naramata Centre has long been on the leading edge of teaching and learning. I wonder what the leading edge will look like in the coming years? Like each step on the labyrinth path, each emerging moment brings an awareness of the edge of our experience. These moments carry us deeper into our true selves.

I trust this is true for Naramata Centre: that this anniversary is simply and profoundly another moment carrying us into our mission, into our true identity, and into discerning what is next for us as God's people. I trust that these moments will weave us always back to the centre.

Allison Rennie
Program Director, Naramata Centre

Naramata village looking south to Penticton

Naramata Morning

If there is a heaven,
*   I am sure it looks like Naramata.*
Flower-filled and bird-blessed,
*   the green softness of the shoulders,*
*   the hips, sloping toward the lake,*
*   liquid circle*
*   cradling fish and waterfowl.*

Lupine, wild rose, lilac, clover,
*   dogs wagging their way down main street,*

*   the rhythmic swoosh of sprinklers,*
*   even in the rain.*

Here breathing is an act of prayer,
*   walking a meditation.*

The loon laughs over the lake
*   and we human beings*
remember
*   who we can become*
*   who we have always known*
*   we are.*

ELIZABETH CARLSON, JUNE 14, 1997

USED BY PERMISSION

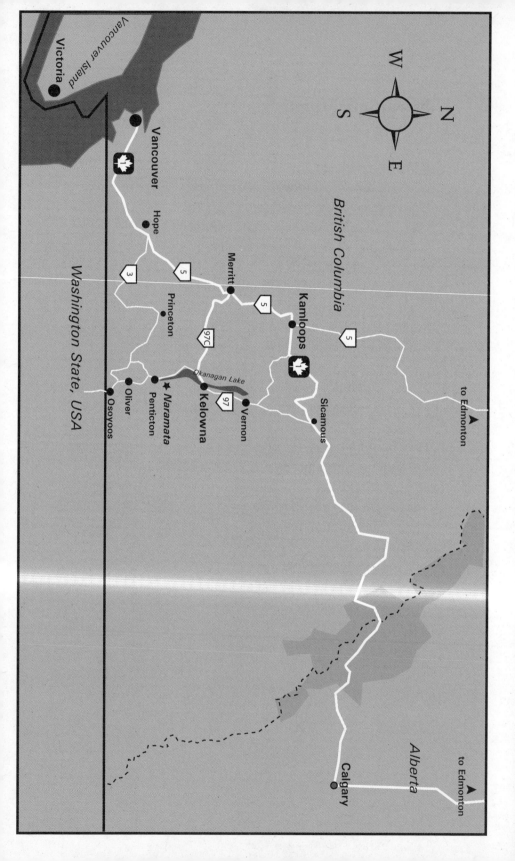

Naramata Centre is located in the heart of Naramata village, about 15 kilometres north of the city of Penticton on the east side of Okanagan Lake, in British Columbia, Canada. The village, established in 1908, sits on a peninsula that juts into the lake. First Nations people, known as Interior Salish (Okanagan Nation), have lived in the area for about nine thousand years. It takes about five hours to drive to Naramata from Vancouver, British Columbia, and nine hours from Calgary, Alberta.

Often described as "a hidden treasure at the end of the road," Naramata village (population 2,500) features peaceful, tree-lined streets perfect for quiet strolls or cycling. The museum and craft shops await those curious about the community's local history and artisans. The Naramata Store provides a variety of groceries, and serves as the community's post office, video outlet, and liquor store, with a country general store welcome. The Naramata Community Church, Village Grounds coffee shop, Camp Creek Station Pub, and Heritage Inn are just some of the local landmarks. Some readers may recall Brent's Dairy Bar (now China Beach) and the delicious fries and ice cream sold there.

Wineries along the Naramata bench offer tours, gift shops, and a selection of award-winning wines. Winding country roads climb high above the lake through local orchards and vineyards and offer picturesque exploring.

The nearby abandoned Kettle Valley Railway, with its dramatic views of Okanagan Lake, attracts thousands of cyclists every year. Hiking trails above the village are a paradise for naturalists and photographers. In the winter, visitors can enjoy cross-country and downhill skiing at nearby ski resorts. There is plenty to explore in Naramata!

Note from the Author

Mary Trainer

I would like to thank everyone who so generously shared their perspectives, memories, and images of Naramata Centre with me. Their unwavering passion and enthusiasm for the centre's purpose, programs, and location are powerful testaments to its decades of success.

Over the summer and fall of 2008, I interviewed dozens of people, combed through 60 years of Board minutes, delighted in reading many back issues of *Good News* and student yearbooks, discovered the wealth of information at the B.C. Conference (Bob Stewart) Archives at the Vancouver School of Theology, and searched for treasure in the dusty cardboard boxes in the basement of McLaren Hall.

The dog-eared photo albums in the foyer of McLaren Hall were a goldmine. Many images from these albums are reproduced in this book and help bring to life people whose experiences at Naramata often resulted in profound and lasting changes in their lives.

This book celebrates what I believe are the centre's historical highlights. With so much research material at hand, and a limited manuscript length, I had to make some difficult choices about what to include. There are dozens more staff members, program resource people, program participants, volunteers, board and committee members, and Naramata village residents whose stories deserve to be told.

I thank my husband, Neil, and daughter, Erin, for their support. I feel grateful and privileged to have had this opportunity to research and write about such an extraordinary place.

Congratulations, Naramata Centre!

Mary D. Trainer

David Giuliano

3250 Bloor Street West
Suite 300
Toronto, Ontario
M8X 2Y4
Canada

Telephone
416-231-7680

Voice Mail
416-231-7680

Toll Free
1-800-268-3781

Fax
416-231-3103

www.united-church.ca

November 24th, 2008

Andrew Church,
Executive Director,
Naramata Centre, Box 68,
Naramata, British Columbia   V0H 1N0

Dear Andrew Church,

On behalf of the church I express deep gratitude for Naramata Centre as The United Church of Canada's treasure in the Okanagan valley. For sixty years it has truly been a place of learning, spiritual insight and support for both lay folks and ministry personnel.

As with all of the United Church education centres, Naramata grew up in the post WWII time of church commitment to lay education and the fostering of lay leadership throughout the church. Inspired by the Iona community in Scotland, our education centres became places of retreat, education, and engagement with the ethical issues of the day. This commitment has not waned over the decades as the centres have been places of action and reflection for succeeding generations of faithful people.

In this vein, the residential Winter Session program for Young Adults has hundreds of graduates who have made important contributions to both church and society and Naramata Centre also plays a significant role in the Youth Ministry certificate program. The dynamic and engaging summer programs provide opportunities for families and individuals to learn and worship together in the tranquil beauty of the Lake Okanagan setting. Sessions in the other three seasons are well known for their creativity and producing some of our Church's most creative leaders. Transformational leadership is a hallmark.

I have always been impressed by the range of programs offered at Naramata. All generations are well served and included in the education and worship life of the Centre. Children and youth are treated with profound respect and their leaders receive excellent leadership training. Parents and grandparents know that the young people are in such good hands that they can relax and indulge in one of their interests whether it is in the arts, physical activities, spiritual practices or ethical engagement.

All this is to say how much the United Church appreciates the wonderful contribution that Naramata has made over the last 60 years and we look forward to many more years of faithful service.

Blessings and peace to you.

David Giuliano (The Right Reverend)
Moderator

MISSION AND
SERVICE FUND

The Mission and Service Fund - supporting United Church work in Canada and around the world
Le fonds "Mission et Service" soutient le travail de l'Eglise Unie au Canada et à travers le monde

Introduction

Naramata Centre continues to be a place of the spirit, inviting people to embark on journeys of self-discovery, and equipping them to take what they learn out into the world.

From the beginning in 1947, the intention of a group of committed western Canadian women and men in the United Church of Canada was to create a welcoming community where young people could relate the gospel of Christ to their lives. It was also to be a place for lay people to take leadership training, and then share that learning with church Sunday schools and the wider community.

It is remarkable that for more than 60 years the original intention has continually met expectations. Naramata Centre has made a difference in the lives of thousands of people, and many hold it dear. Many have been challenged, nurtured, and renewed. The experiences shared in this book testify to the deep affection the centre garners and to the gratitude felt for what happens in a place that invites and supports exploration – both inside and out.

I have asked myself how the centre continues to be "on the edge," and am convinced that it results from a long-standing commitment and flexibility on the part of Board and Committee members, program participants, volunteers, and staff to embrace the founding intention by welcoming people of all faiths and nationalities; paying attention to issues in the wider world; taking risks in programming; and honouring children and youth more deeply. The centre's innovative leadership and teamwork have contributed greatly to keeping that edge during six decades of profound technological and societal change.

During my research, I heard repeatedly that Naramata Centre is a "safe" place. In a way, being "safe" is the antithesis of being "on the edge." Yet this safe place provides the base from which people can leap into growth, learning, and new experiences.

Many people talked about the very tangible presence of spirit in this place. Staff and volunteers acknowledged a deep sense of being accompanied by God in their work and life at Naramata Centre. The centre's ability to renew itself so that it continues to be relevant to current needs will require ongoing discernment of God's call.

The Capital Campaign launched in 2007 to "restore, refresh and create" concretely demonstrates the centre's commitment to a healthy future. The more enduring commitment to young people and leadership training that began in 1947 lives on through all those who have experienced this magical place and are inspired to make a difference in the world.

Mary D. Trainer
Penticton, 2008

a dream becomes reality

*It's something of a miracle
to come to understand yourself.*
~ ALLEEN MCLAREN

An Adventure in Faith

In the years immediately following World War II, society changed rapidly. New technologies unfolded and a generation of liberated young people were free to live their lives much differently from their parents.

Challenging questions arose for church leaders. Did the church have something meaningful and relevant to say to this new generation? Were there trained and experienced leaders able to meet youth "just where they were"? Could the gospel of Christ be shown as relevant to their lives?

C. R. MacGillivray

"These questions all came home to me more forcefully when I became the minister of the Penticton United Church in the Okanagan Valley in 1937," wrote C. R. MacGillivray. Although the teacher training courses offered by the church at that time were helpful, MacGillivray felt there was something lacking. An idea came to him. What if there could be a school for leadership training in his own Presbytery that addressed the questions?

Although he was Convenor of the Christian Education Committee of the Okanagan Presbytery, MacGillivray didn't mention the idea to the Presbytery Committee, but on his own began to search for a site. An abandoned Baptist school on the bench between Summerland and Penticton in the south Okanagan was available, but had no beach. Union College in Vancouver, B.C., which had ample facilities and was vacant during the summer season, was also evaluated. "However, careful consideration showed that neither Union College nor any other site within the bounds of a large centre would offer requirement necessary to assure success in the initial venture," wrote MacGillivray. Because he was so familiar with the Okanagan Valley, he turned his attention to Naramata "because of its climate, splendid beaches and removal from any large centre."

Support for the school was not limited to MacGillivray. He was elected Chair of the B.C. Conference Christian Education Committee, which unanimously supported his vision. Roy Stobie (minister at Penticton United Church from 1944 to 1949), R. A. (Bob) McLaren (Field Secretary[1] of Christian Education for the B.C. Conference), Clyde Woollard (a youth worker in the United Church), and Charlie Burritt (Chair of *As One That Serves* – a United Church men's group) were directly involved. Individual women and women's groups got behind the idea too.[2]

Roy Stobie's daughter Jean recalls,

There was indeed much thought and searching both outer and inner involved, and I well remember my mother feeding and housing Bob and Charlie so that the three could spend time deep in thought about how this might all come into being. There was NO money, so one of the great stories is of my dad going to the train station in Penticton to pick up these two, both very big men, coming from Vancouver to find them both sharing a single bunk!

The members of the committee were convinced that all students should live in residence and share study, fellowship, and play. They envisioned a place where students freely and openly discussed the relevance of Christ to their lives. They continued to work to finalize a site location and to find a school principal. At this point, Bob McLaren volunteered to be the principal if he was appointed pastor of the Naramata pastorate. MacGillivray wrote,

This was a real breakthrough for the committee. The recommendation forthwith was made to the N.N. Committee[3] and the Naramata Church that Mr. McLaren should, if possible, be placed in charge of the Naramata pastorate. This being done, a recommendation was made to the Conference that steps be taken at the earliest moment to lay the foundations for beginning a Christian Leadership Training School centred at Naramata.

In May 1947, the following resolution was adopted by the Conference:

Whereas, at the Annual Meeting of the B.C. Conference in 1946, a special committee was set up to organize and establish a Leadership Training School, and, whereas we have heard a comprehensive report of the steps and means taken to that end – This Conference therefore most heartily endorses the action of their committee and approves the plans which have been formulated. We furthermore concur in their choice of the Rev. Robert A. McLaren, as Dean of said Training School. We further pledge our support in assuring recruits for leadership training in this school, and lastly, this conference, realizing that such a school is an adventure of deep faith to meet a dire need in our Church, we do ask for the good will and prayers of every United Church member in our Conference.

That same spring, MacGillivray and McLaren travelled to Toronto where the Committee's recommendations were adopted by the Christian Education Board. Once back in B.C., McLaren began publicizing the new school through United Church congregations in western Canada. The response was immediate and encouraging. A board of directors was then appointed, chaired by Mortimer Lees. The dream of Naramata Christian Leadership School was a reality at last.

First Board of the Christian Leadership Training School
back, l to r: Bert Whitmore, Bill Nicholl, Max Warne, Roy Stobie, S.V.H. Redman
front, l to r: Bob McLaren, G.B. Switzer, M.W. Lees

Setting a

NEW PATTERN IN TRAINING

for Lay Leadership

THE NEW BUILDING . . . Now nearing completion

OFFICIAL OPENING
November 3rd, 1948

CHRISTIAN LEADERSHIP
TRAINING SCHOOL

Naramata, B. C.

UNITED CHURCH OF CANADA

Official Opening, 1948

Four hundred guests attended the opening ceremony of the school on November 3, 1948. Norman MacKenzie, President of the University of British Columbia, officially opened the school and R. P. Stobie, Chairman of the school's Board of Managers, gave the benediction.

PENTICTON HERALD

The South Okanagan's Daily Newspaper

This building is a most interesting project, achieved entirely by voluntary support, a dream partially realized, and which offers endless opportunities for further co-operative effort.

By the most careful and inspired planning and tremendous efforts of a handful of workers, the various gifts from the friends of the school have been co-ordinated into a building and furnishings, incomplete, yet adequate to house thirty students together with the staff and to carry on the work of this, the second term of the school.

The rooms have been furnished in the bare necessities: beds, chests of drawers, desks and chairs and drapes. These have been bought wholesale at a cost of $87 per room, which accommodates two students.

Many donations such as fruit, vegetables, jams, household items and many other articles were received during the afternoon.

The Penticton Herald covered the event.

The Early Years

Zeal. Hospitality. Pleasure. Congratulations. Such words are sprinkled throughout the board minutes during the early years. In November 1952, McLaren enthusiastically reported to the board that in five years, the school had gone from a hostel with one wash basin to being worth about $175,000. It had hosted 196 winter students; the number of "friends" had zoomed to 1002, and donations continued to pour in.

Cost to run Naramata Centre
- **the first year: about $17,000**
- **in 1977: $577,550**
- **in 2007: $2,568,785**

Alvin Cooper, a representative from the Board of Christian Education in Toronto, continued to bring the United Church of Canada's support to the school. In 1952 he appeared before the board with an invigorated message that stated, "Religion has been crowded into a smaller and smaller segment of life, and out of the ashes of hopes all across the world have come lay impulses to repair this lack." One such "lay impulse" was to create centres like Naramata which "have caught the imagination of the church and tend to bind Conferences together."

The same year, the Prairie Christian Training School was established in Qu'Appelle, Saskatchewan; in 1953 another school, Five Oaks, opened in Paris, Ontario. Work was also underway on the Atlantic Christian Training Centre in Tatamagouche, Nova Scotia, which opened in 1955.

Cooper concluded his 1952 visit with these words.

I am persuaded it (the "centre" movement) means more than we dream. I am convinced it can mean great things in the avocation of a Christian. The church is wherever a Christian is working and the Kingdom of God is being built where Christians are working and serving. We seek to educate not only the mind but the heart, the dynamic of spiritual consciousness in the soul, the awareness of the motivation of God in the soul of each student.

Co-founders Bob and Alleen McLaren with son Kenneth on Bob's knee; back row,
l to r: children Betty, Bobby, Edwin

Co-founder Bob McLaren tells his story

The following text is taken from a typed document, dated 1983.

I was born and brought up on the Prairies - Crossfield and Bowden, Alberta. I know something of the hardships and struggles of the Prairie pioneer people. I inherited two things; how to be practical and make do without almost any money.

A sense of warmth and hospitality (born of hardship) that was such an outstanding characteristic of the Prairie people, not only of Alberta but across the West.

I became a teacher and taught for three years. This really led me into the ministry. I felt if I could help to "light a fire" in a young person's LIFE there would be no limit to what they might do with their life.

After ordination, I served two short two-year (2-year) terms in Alberta. Because I was from Alberta, I was familiar with the centres for Lay Persons operated by the Sects: Three Hills, Briar Crest and the Mennonites at Didsbury. We had only our Theological School and University, but no place to send laypersons, boys or girls or older people to find out who they really were, and get some training and understanding to help them take leadership in their Church and community.

I was then appointed as Field Secretary for Christian Education for B.C. - July 1943 - After serving in this capacity for four years I felt as did others that we should have a Lay Training Centre and if others could do it we certainly could too.

There were others in our Province that strongly
felt that we needed a place for lay training. Rev.
Harrison Villett, Dr. Gerry Switzer, Dr. Doug Telfer,
Rev. Roy Stobie, Rev. Charlie MacGillivray, to mention
only a few.

About this time we were
extremely fortunate to get Dr.
Clyde Woollard on the Christian
Education staff helping on
the field staff as a Boys Work
Secretary. He did a great deal
in the planning of the Centre
and later on the staff at the
Centre. Roy Stobie did much on
the board and then came on the
staff at the Centre later.

There were many laymen who
played a very important part:
Guy Flavelle, Jack Robinson,
Charlie Burrett, Roy Johnson,
Dr. Harry Grant, to mention
only a few.

Clyde Woollard

We had some real difficulties to solve. We did not
have a pattern to follow that was of our Church. Did
not know where to start.

We didn't have any students lined up for sure, or
staff, and we did not have any money.

Each time we approached our B.C. Conference for help
and permission to start. They felt it would not work
and would only become a White Elephant in our church.
Even the Board of Christian Education in Toronto, the
head office of our Church, thought and said that it
would not work.

Finally the B.C. Conference said to me, "Bob, if you go out and get 2 or even $3000.00 you can make a beginning." In three weeks I had $9000.00. They were pleased and surprised, mostly surprised.

I did not want to leave my work as Field Secretary of Christian Education so we tried to get someone to be the principal or director of this new Centre. But because they were anxious about assurance of salary and where to live and travel expenses – we could not promise anything for sure.

I resigned as Field Secretary in July 1947, and became the Principal of what we then called The Christian Leadership Training School at Naramata. We had no assurance of any money except just what we could raise from friends or persons or groups we could interest.

Phyllis Stobie, first secretary at the school, and daughter Catherine, future board chair and director of the Healing Pathway

We went to Naramata, near Penticton, where Roy Stobie was minister in the United Church. Alleen, my wife, along with our two little children were not afraid to enter into this new venture.

We rented a little house in Naramata as our first home there, and I became the minister of the Naramata Church. The only money we were absolutely sure of was the $500.00 a year I got for being the minister.

We had, I think, 32 students the first year. They lived in a rented Hostel owned by the Fruit Packing House. Some of the students worked in the packing house until Christmas, and then our courses began after Christmas in the basement of the Naramata Church.

I was the only member on the staff except for Phyllis Stobie (now Mrs. Campbell) who was made secretary.

All the teaching was done by ministers who donated their time, and came to us from different parts of the province. It only cost us their transportation and their food. We bought a little empty building about 12' x 24' from the airport, and moved it into the Church property, as we did not own anything and we used it for the Secretary. Later it was used as a Craft Shop for the Students.

We couldn't really buy anything. We either got it given to us or we did without. A typewriter was given to us that was partly damaged by fire, and we sent a letter to the women's groups in our Church across B.C., Alberta and Saskatchewan. The response was beautiful. The Centre will be forever indebted to the women of our Church. Many of these little groups did not know where we were or what the word meant, some thought it was a Japanese word. Some letters came back and said things like this: "We don't know just where you are, or what you will teach, but we all think you will do something for our young people." "Please accept this $15.00 from our small group in Northern Saskatchewan." With the help of these United Church women the Centre has never looked back and we went on from strength to strength.

The war [WWII] was over and army buildings were available as were beds and mattresses, cooking pots and kitchen equipment, benches, etc.

Jack Robinson, our layman from Ryerson Church in Vancouver, put down $250.00 as a deposit on a huge OFFICERS QUARTERS AND MESS building in Vernon until our little board could meet and talk about it. We decided to act and bought the whole building for I think $3000.00, had it taken apart for about $3000.00, and carried down on trucks for about $2500.00 (30 truck loads about 5 tons each).

We then got Hugh Dobson who was our friend, and the son of Dr. Hugh Dobson of the United Church. Hugh Jr. was an architect who had done outstanding work for, I think, Bental Construction. He came to Naramata and drew the first building, using the material and the same lumber lengths from the army building. This building is now known at the School as McLaren Hall. The total cost

Early McLaren Hall

for his services was $24.00 which was the train fare to
Penticton and back from Vancouver.

Many mills never gave us money, but did give lumber. One mill gave us 6000 feet every year for about 6
years. Guy Flavelle of Flavelle Cedar, gave us all the
cedar siding we could use. A boy I was in College with
from Alberta gave us an International Tractor.
W. Schnell from Camrose, Alberta, gave us a truck.

Canning area at the school

A firm in Armstrong gave us all the split peas we
could use, and Sonny Boy firm in Camrose gave us quanti-
ties of cereal.

We put in our own canning equipment, and the students came early and helped in Work Camps, and did most of the canning.

A student, Eleanor Ferguson, came to us from the Peace River. She knew how to print – i.e. run Platen presses. We put in our own presses, one 6x12 and one 12x15, this was followed by a Multilith press.

If Bob found a doorknob, he'd build a house around it!

~ CAMPUS SAYING

Because we had our own paper cutters and presses, we got Barber Ellis to give us one ton of fine paper a year.

There was hardly any end to the gifts we got. When money was given to us we made every dollar do the work of three. Anybody can spend money. But how far can you make it go? Because we made it do so much, people did not mind helping, in fact they took real joy out of being part of helping others, especially youth.

There was one who made a very large gift when we were building our first building, and he said "this is all I'm going to give, I don't plan to give any more, any year". He ended up giving every year and when he died gave something like $100,000 to the Centre.

People stayed with us through the years. I think people stayed with us because we did such an honest, reliable job with everything that was given to us. Some gifts were large, some were small. Every gift was important, very important. It was most appreciated, not only by those of us who received and administered it, but by the thousands who were helped by it.

I remember one day receiving a letter from a woman in Northern Alberta. The letter had two "one dollar bills" and this note. "I'm old now, 82, and I have some arthritis, but I can still knit. I have knitted two pairs of socks and sold them for $1.00 each. I want you to have the $2.00 for your school." I was touched by that letter. How could I ever spend any gift unless it was in such a light of this spirit and prayer. For while I pinned the letter and the $2.00 up on my wall, I wasn't in any way able to spend it.

I think people helped because we had such a spirit of hospitality. It was no credit to me that I had it. I simply inherited it. It was part of my life, it was not possible for me to ask in any other way. It was THE SPIRIT OF OUR HOME AND THE SPIRIT OF ALL THE OTHER HOMES THAT I KNEW ON THE PRAIRIES.

No one was ever turned away because they lacked the funds. This went for the courses - Summer or Winter. Sometimes a young married couple wanted to take the winter courses for the six months. They were given a free cottage if they needed it. A whole family could take a summer course if they needed to do it this way.

We did not plan to make much on the running of the Centre, but rather we planned to get help from outside the School, both in materials and in money.

Naramata will always need financial help from outside. No Educational or even Medical Centre can operate from fees alone. It needs help from those of us outside.

I am sure people will feel now as they did when we were in the beginning of the Centre. Glad to be a part of helping others go on to meaningful things for to- morrow, and every to-morrow.

It is very true — the thing that you give away is yours forever and forever. It goes on from strength to strength to strength — in Others.

Co-founder Alleen McLaren tells her story

Alleen McLaren

I was personally committed to the establishment of the Leadership Training School at Naramata. Having attended the United Church Training School for Women in Toronto, I knew first-hand the values of opportunities for spiritual and intellectual achievement, and I wanted to do my part to give that opportunity to others.[4]

I was very much in tune with the establishment of the school. I wanted everyone to have the kind of interpretation of the Bible that the staff and church leaders had.

When we first moved to Naramata from Vancouver, we lived in a little shack across from where the centre now stands, but only for a month. Later, a very kind woman, Mrs. Ruth Rounds, let us rent a home that she owned on the main street.

While I was able to see the growth of students at the school, I was also aware of how Naramata shaped the attitudes of our own children. We really 'lived' with the students. They were a part of our family. They did their washing in my machine in the kitchen. They played with our children. My daughter, Betty, was in kindergarten when we moved to Naramata. Jean Jamieson was the resident student pianist, and she and Jean Jefferson, the violinist, were the people who helped to lead the children's work. Betty was in that group and had the benefit of these associations.

That first fall and winter, the men and women of Naramata United Church assisted both students and staff; they hosted receptions, offered the hospitality of their homes, and even housecleaned the packing house hostel where our students were to live that first year. The students worked hard all summer and fall earning money in the fruit orchards and on the assembly line packing fruit. By January, we began classes in the basement of the United Church, and although we had by that time acquired laundry equipment, a piano, and some furniture, those first winter session students and staff had to overlook many material inadequacies.

I was there through 17 years with the student body, and then when Ivan Cumming came as principal, he asked me to come back in the human relations movement to work in the laboratories[5] where you came to see yourself in terms of your relationship in the community. I was glad to be a part of that. It helped me in my place in society, because I moved into a feminist period of seeing life in terms of being a woman who was involved in her own right. And this human relations movement helped me with that.

At the time it [Naramata Centre] was founded, I thought of myself as a partner. I certainly kept the home together – we raised four children. I saw that as my part. Also, I did all the entertaining the first few years. Visitors came from Vancouver and had their dinner in our home. And I didn't have any hired help other than what I hired myself as help. So, from the point of view outside now, I look on myself as a founder.

BOB MCLAREN WAS BORN IN 1910 AND DIED IN 1998.
ALLEEN MCLAREN WAS BORN IN 1919 AND LIVES IN VICTORIA, B.C.

The lawns of Naramata
A robe of living green
Disclose to use the secrets
Of things that are not seen:
The grove that lifts its bosom,
The lake behind its shade
Reveal to us the loveliness
Of all things God has made.

The skies of Naramata
Envelop and adorn
The splendour of the evening,
The coolness of the morn
Unbounded in their glory
That changes hour by hour
They tell an age-old story
Of wonder and of power.

The hearts of Naramata
Human and grave and gay,
A joy to all who've known them
Inspire us on our way:
From them we learn to labour,
To search the Sacred Word,
To love our every neighbour
And witness for our Lord.

W. J. ROSE, 1955

A Beautiful Setting In The Okanagan Valley

A Tradition In Excellence Since 1947

A WINTER SESSION FOR YOUNG ADULTS [18 - 24]

Asking the Questions of Heart, Mind & Soul

1. WHERE DO I GO FROM HERE?
2. WHAT WORK DO I WANT TO DO?
3. HOW WILL I LEAVE HOME?
4. WHAT LIFESTYLE WILL I CHOOSE?
5. WHAT'S REALLY WORTH IT?
6. AM I LOVABLE AND COMPETENT?
7. WHO WILL I LOVE?

8. IN WHAT DO I BELIEVE?
9. IN WHOM DO I BELIEVE?
10. WHAT DIFFERENCE DOES BEING A MAN OR A WOMAN MAKE?
11. HOW DO I MAKE DECISIONS ABOUT MY SEXUALITY?
12. HOW WILL I SURVIVE IN THE SOCIETY OF THE 90's?
13. AM I RESPONSIBLE?

14. IS ANYBODY LISTENING?

naramata Centre

A Five Month Residential Community Learning Experience

Freedom To Discover Your Own Questions And Answers

winter session

It is truly amazing to realise that this core program continues to be offered since the centre began in 1947. I believe that Winter Session is unique in offering one of the most significant learning experiences at that crucial time in a young adult's life. It also provides a huge learning challenge for the leaders and for the leaders' partners and families, who cannot help but change and grow as well.

~ Mary Robertson

Winter Session. Four months of basic Christian training for young people. That was the purpose of the Christian Leadership Training School when it opened to the first students in 1947. Principal Bob McLaren asserted that "the basic training will deepen and enrich your own religious life, and make you a valuable servant in doing God's work all the rest of your life."

Winter Session has evolved gradually over six decades. From the early goal of equipping students for a life in Christian leadership, the centre now aims to equip them for a spirit-filled life of self-awareness, healthy relationships, and leadership. In the 1940s, Winter Session courses were geared to empowering students to go into church congregations to support education and leadership.[1] As society shifted, and the church's relationship to society also shifted, the nature of the courses changed. In the 1960s, topics included sensitivity training; Christian understanding of sex, love and marriage; and alcohol education. By the late 1970s, more courses reflected contemporary themes and included transactional analysis, the environment and the Third World, decision making and goal setting, gestalt, comparative religions, and death and dying. The influence of the experiential model in the 1970s and 1980s meant students learned more through reflecting on experiences than from lectures on theology and Bible study.

Winter Session fees:	
1947–48	none
1963	$330
2008	$3,850

Bob Wallace (staff associate) comes in to give a lecture and starts by saying, "We all have a job to do. Yours is to sit and listen and mine is to stand and give this lecture. If you finish before I do, put up your hand."

~ FROM THE 1961 HIGH CARD

For example, in the early and mid-1980s, Winter Session students lived for a week in Vancouver's downtown eastside. They experienced first-hand people struggling with homelessness, poverty, and physical and mental illness, and investigated social systems, resources, and politics.

Today, Winter Session continues the traditions of the past where needs and interests of the participants give shape to the program curriculum. The learning environment is based on four big questions: Who am I? Who am I in relationship? Who am I in the world? Who am I in my spirit? In the intersection between these questions and each group member Winter Session content is formed. Program director Allison Rennie explains.

> In 2004 we had a group of young people who were very politically active, thoughtful, and interested. Their passion was being engaged with the world...That year we were at peace rallies and International Women's Day celebrations. We did things that took us into the community in ways that made sense for that group.
>
> In 2008, we had a group that was much more interested and excited about spirituality. We ended up doing a six-week series on virtues to cover the period of Lent. Every week of Lent, we had a different virtue (patience, compassion, and so on) that became a focus for that week. We were still out in the community, but the whole tone of that Winter Session was related to the needs of those particular students.

Since 1980, average attendance at Winter Session has been 15–20 people.

Former centre director Mary Robertson recalls Winter Session program participants brainstorming and negotiating the topics for study, with clowning being one popular choice.

> I recall the challenge of taking our silent clowns to the elementary school in Naramata, and to the malls of Penticton. There was also an outreach requirement, to encourage participants to give service in the Naramata and Penticton communities. The options included reading to visually impaired seniors, assisting in a seniors' swim program, assisting in a children's early development program, and helping

the centre with whatever was needed on the grounds, in the kitchen, and in the office."

Still, the centre applies four main themes to all Winter Sessions, regardless of who shows up: learning communication skills; developing self-awareness; being equipped with tools to build and maintain healthy relationships; and receiving models for thinking about the world and how it works.

> **Winter Session now runs from January to April every other year.**

In the Beginning

The dean gave the courses the first year, assisted by church ministers from around the province. Field secretaries lectured on practical phases of the educational work of the church. Thirty-five full-time students attended the first Winter Session.

The first classes were held at the United Church.

Classes were held in the basement of the little United Church in Naramata. The church was taken over by the packing house and demolished in 1981, but there is a sign on the side of the packing house indicating where it used to stand.

The church, built in 1911, was originally Methodist.

In the fall of 1947 (and prior to the start of Winter Session), students came to Naramata and worked in the packing house sorting the culls from the good fruit. Rent was deducted from salaries. When the packing house closed for the season, negotiations with the packing house allowed students to continue living on the property during Winter Session (January to April) 1948.

Syndica House

Girls stayed in a hostel (Syndica House) at the northwest end of the packing house property. A ladies committee from the school equipped the hostel with linoleum mats for all the rooms, runners for the halls, curtains, and miscellaneous furniture. Boys and married couples lived in the community.

If they hadn't arrived earlier to work in the packing plant, all students were encouraged to participate in work camp, starting mid-October. The Ascent Yearbook of 1963 conveys this comprehensive description of work camp.

> By the 15th of October, 1962, most of those who were to become the class of 1962–63 were on campus ready for hard labor...although most of the jobs: gardening, canning, building and ground clean-up, and painting etc., were mundane and monotonous, they were approached in a mood of questioning excitement. Everyone wanted to know why everyone else had come, where they had come from, whether they were glad they had come.

Work camp duties, 1953

In the evening, Rev. R. Wallace held sway in front of the fireplace in the Lounge at Columbia Hall. In these "Orientation Lectures" Bob talked about the various things the school had in mind for us, our status within the community and our responsibility to it in the form of skippers, study, assignments, and worship. He also talked about 'Christian Vocation' and 'Love' (not luv). We got into quick and active discussion after these talks. He also introduced us to his idiosyncrasy of reading passages from good books by good authors. The most dramatic, during work camp, was a lengthy reading from *The Bomb that Fell on America* by H. Hagdorn. Each day was closed with a vesper led by various members of the staff. This was an unusual practise for most of us, and the morning worship was even more alien, to the extent that many of us were self-conscious and uneasy about it. However, many accepted this and came to appreciate Christ as a worthy part of their life at the school. These morning worships were an introduction to Dr. McLaren.

A work camp gets maintenance and some capital construction work done for the school, but of much greater importance, it provides the environment for strangers to mix and talk with each other. Everyone sized up their new acquaintances, with particular concern for those of the opposite gender. Staff and faculty were scrutinized just as closely and critically with pressure on personal prejudices concerning age, cultural and educational differences. Not a week had gone by before most of us were jolted out of our complacencies and left hanging, completely bewildered about each other and about the philosophies behind the operation of the school.

So ended Work Camp. And so we turned to the Winter Course proper.

Students were not exempt from chores during Winter Session either. Intricately bound up with the life of the school were the "skippers" – students who were given jobs from washing floors to chopping wood.

Student Chris Grauer recalls that in Winter Session 1968–69, there were only two cooks and 33 of us. So we had to help peel vegetables, set up for meals, serve the meals, and do the dishes afterwards, because the cooks worked split shift. We all enjoyed that. It gave a bit of break from the "head" stuff. We also had work camps on Saturday. We washed our own linen — wringer washers — and by a year missed having to shovel coal in the furnace for heat.

Many years ago, Bruce and Kathleen Hatfield of Calgary, Alberta, told their four daughters that they would give each of them four years of post secondary education. Barb, Kate, Linda, and Sue Hatfield chose to use one year of their education taking Winter Session. They all graduated, the last in 1981. "It was the best," recalls Sue. "It's an education that you can't get in another institution."

And from David Thompson, staff member Winter Session 1976: We are now in our fourth week. Almost everyone still comes to sessions, and almost everyone has started missing breakfast. In brief, we've raked leaves, dug flower beds, cleared the creek bed, gone to the tunnel, done awareness exercises, practiced communication skills, examined the way we want to live together, sung, formed a recorder group, studied the Bible, practiced group process skills, spent hours deciding what to do with the final 12 weeks, worshipped, worked through at least 946 decisions, done batik, painting, pottery, macramé, and creative movement, played badminton, tried to get the washing machine to wash our clothes. And spent many hours talking. Sharing and caring, and sometimes fighting.

After Sunday evening church services, students welcomed a taste of home life when they were invited into homes of staff or people in the community.

Everything's not rosy and cozy, but we're learning to deal with differences in a way that allows for both individual and community needs.

The following excerpt from *The Gateway* (1952) describes a typical student day at Winter Session.

7:15 a.m. Rise and shine! Occasionally there is the sound of little feet pattering over the floors. These are the servers who are wandering about trying to get their eyes open by the time the serving bell rings, so that too many dishes won't get broken.

7:30 a.m. Serving bell. Everyone up. "Come, come gang, you will be late for breakfast. Get up!"

Mrs. Packham, Dean of Women, 1959

7:45 a.m. Breakfast. "Okay, stay in bed and see if we care." They're off! Don and Dale, that is. "Don't forget your lunch, fellows."

8:15 a.m. Fags.[2] Tote that mop, push that broom. Keep on going 'fore Ish lowers the boom.

8:45 a.m. Quiet time. The most important half hour of the day, when we take time for meditation and communion with God. On nice days most of us go down to the lakeshore or out on quiet, lonely paths.

9:15 a.m. First lecture. Whether it is a lecture on Paul, on the Life of Jesus or Christian Education, we give our wholehearted attention to our lecturer.

10:05 a.m. Second lecture. Either Miss Simpson is teaching us the great prayers of the Bible, and how to better use our time for personal devotions, or Mr. McLaren is making us "unbend" in his Public Speaking Class.

10:50 a.m. Morning break. All make a mad dash to see who got letters and food parcels and during this time we also get in a quick game of volley ball or softball.

11:15 a.m. Third lecture. Back to our notebooks for some fast writing to keep up with our visiting lecturer. They have so much valuable information to give us that we don't want to miss any of it.

12:00 a.m. Serving bell. The time when a few opinions about the lectures are exchanged and pleasant aromas float from the kitchen.

12:15 p.m. Lunch. We are all so famished that we just dig in and few words are exchanged at first. Of course towards the end of the meal the conversation picks up considerably and we enjoy a real mealtime fellowship.

12:45 p.m. Dishes. Oftentimes sour notes are thrown around the kitchen at this time. Luckily, though, very few dishes are.

1:30 p.m. Study period. Notes are recopied and assignments are begun. Some even manage to finish them.

4:00 p.m. Craft period. Some of us tear our hair, sand our fingers, shellac our clothes as we struggle valiantly with trays, bowls and magazine racks in the craftshop with Clay's patient assistance, while others learn perseverance the hard way in shell-craft, figurine painting and glitter-bird making in the dining room under Miss Simpson's capable supervision.

5:15 p.m. Servers' bell. Everyone running to get cleaned up for supper. "Why doesn't that shellac come off easier?"

5:30 p.m. Supper. Sue, how do you do it? You are an absolute genius to make such delectable meals for us all the time. We raise our hats to you!

6:00 p.m. Dishes again. Oh me! I'm afraid the novelty is wearing off a bit.

6:45 p.m.   Another study period – regular assignments completed and extras kept up to date – supplementary reading, prayer, poem, song and game collections.

9:00 p.m.   Sing-song. Whether it's a non-sense song or a spiritual we all put our hearts and voices into it. It has been noticed that we haven't sung "Peter" often since Brian got all "diffused" when he led it.

9:15 p.m.   Vespers in the quiet of the evening hour – and as each night a student or staff member voices his own meditations and thoughts on some well-loved subject, the benediction of God's grace and love descends to us gathered in the comfortable common room before the warmly blazing fire, and the friendship circle at the close draws us all closer in a common fellowship.

9:30 p.m.   Free time. Over a cup of cocoa small discussion groups form, or we step out for a breath of fresh air before retiring for the evening.

10:45 p.m.   Lights out.

11:00 p.m.   LIGHTS OUT I say![3]

Christian Leadership Training School Pennant

"YOUTH ON TOUR"

STUDENTS of UNITED CHURCH

Christian Leadership Training School

NARAMATA, B.C.

Through the Peace River!

TOUR PERSONNEL

Left to Right

Rev. R. A. McLAREN, Principal
MISS M. WOURNELL, Edmonton
MR. O. J. ANDERSON, Nelson Forest District
MRS. O. J. ANDERSON, Nelson Forest District
MR. JIM MITTEN, Vancouver

Played Trumpet with Kitsilano Boys Band

Trained Lay Leadership Makes the Church More Effective!

Meet and Hear Representatives of Your School

PLACE: _____

DATE: _____ APRIL 1951

The Tours

When Winter Session ended, it was time for the tours to set off. Small groups, each with a staff member as a guide, travelled to particular destinations in British Columbia and Alberta so that congregations could hear of the school's work. A major purpose of the tours was to recruit students for the coming year. At the same time, friends could catch up on the latest news, and the visiting students had a chance to put into practise the leadership skills they had learned during the winter. Congregation members billeted the students, who were eager to make new contacts and share their experiences.

In the early years, the students travelled in a cream-coloured bus; in later years, they travelled in their own or borrowed cars.

Tour Bus

He [Bob Mclaren] was good on the campaign trail. He was ...very optimistic... he was used to being in the public.

~ SARAH MORGAN (NEE BARTNER)

F. E. Runnalls, a minister in Armstrong, British Columbia, provides insight into the warmth and character of one of the first tours.

> ...The young people of our church in Armstrong served a supper and, with introductions and singing, enjoyed the happy fellowship. The students gave a public evening programme with recitations, solos, violin solo, a religious play and some brief speeches on the work of the school...the students transmitted to the audience a warm feeling which was an expression of their own spiritual experience and beyond words to describe...The impression left upon our congregation was tremendous.

In 1956, Principal McLaren asked students Charles Clotworthy and Bob Bell if they would like to try a new tour that would include the northern communities and some First Nations communities on the west coast of British Columbia. Bob Bell relates:

> This tour, which took us three weeks to complete, followed Highway 16 from Prince George through the Cariboo and on to the coastal town of Ocean Falls. Here we were met by Rev. Jack Towers, skipper of the United Church mission boat *Thomas Crosby*, and enlisted (were shanghaied?) to serve as his crew. For the next two weeks, we sailed through the inner passage of the West Coast calling in at Klemtu, Bull Harbour, Bella Bella, Bella Coola, other smaller communities, and lighthouses. Charles and I gave many church services and talks on this trip, made possible by the church collections and hospitality of people we met along the way.

Testimonials from Winter Session Graduates

>> I spent hours out in the hills around Naramata meditating and pondering what I was learning. It opened up the Bible to me in a new way. I learned to get along with people of different backgrounds and outlooks, deepened my faith, and gained the ability to go on questioning and seeking.

ANITA GREENAWAY (NEE STEWART; CLASS OF 1948)

>> I came to Naramata after spending three unsuccessful years at the University of British Columbia, which created more problems than anything else. Many of my expectations, therefore, concerned [finding] solutions to these problems. To be honest, I did not enjoy life at Naramata at all until the last two weeks when I discovered that you must risk, even if you lose, in order to live successfully. The course content, the staff, and the type of friendship that can be found if one tries, are all fantastic. It has been a worthwhile experience, and I hope it is just the beginning for me.

CHRIS GRAUER (CLASS OF 1968)

>> Winter Session was perfect for the time of transition between youth and adulthood. For most students, it was the first time living away from home, and all that meant... The program we all helped design filled in the gaps that our formal schooling had left and we were empowered to question, determine our own path, and practice and reflect on new ideas and experiences.

It was the right place at the right time.

~ BARBARA HATFIELD & ALISON ADAMS NELNER

Transactional analysis, human relations training labs, women's and men's consciousness raising and other trendy behaviour theories and practices gave us tools for developing healthy relationships in our personal and professional lives. At that time, we felt we were "cutting edge" and making new discoveries about how people relate to one another. It gave us a language and a framework for effective communication.

Winter Session gave us the time and resources to pursue creative outlets. Personal gifts and talents were discovered and enthusiastically nurtured through potting, painting, playwriting, photography, music making, and more. It is also reassuring to know that our experience at Winter Session continues to provide us, as mid-lifers, with skills and understanding.

As a group of young people striving to live intentionally in Christian community, there were many opportunities to experience spirit at work. For two young women from the "wilderness" of suburban Calgary, Winter Session was time in a cocooned oasis, a Garden of Eden of sorts. The trees laden with fruit, the refreshing lake waters, and the quiet, reflective, protected environment made it unique. We will never forget the rich and fertile ground it provided, the blessing of the relationships that grew, and the many ways in which our spirits were nourished.

Barbara Hatfield & Alison Adams Nelner (class of 1976)

>> Relationships are an integral component of life, defining who we are and how we relate to everything. Fittingly, relationship was a major theme during Winter Session 2008. We were introduced to this theme on our first night together with a call and response reading of the following quote by Australian Aboriginal activist, Lilla Watson:
If you have come here to help me, you are wasting your time. But if you have come here because your liberation is bound up with mine, then let us work together.

Watson's words helped to encourage an environment of gentleness, safety, and support at Winter Session, and were often repeated as a reminder of a common purpose to grow together.

Going into Winter Session I felt unable to relate with others my age; I felt separate. Thus I had a strong desire to connect with my peers. They helped me understand that I am worthy of relationships with others my age. As a result, I had to stop blam-

Winter Session students hamming it up, 1991

ing God, the world, and my peers for my perceived situation and forgive my belief in unworthiness. The completion of my goal was one of joy, and one I could never have accomplished without support from my Winter Session companions.

Throughout Winter Session I also supported my companions' transcendence of their own personal challenges. This too was a joyful experience for me. It was the miracle of recognizing that my liberation was bound up with theirs and theirs with mine.

RYAN JAMES (CLASS OF 2008)

W.J. "Uncle Bill" Rose

Uncle Bill

Of all the people I met and lived with at Naramata Centre, William John Rose (1885–1968) was perhaps the most remarkable. Uncle Bill, as he was known, was living out his retirement in Rose Cottage beside Columbia Hall. He was a mentor to all and his unpretentious demeanour belied his remarkable life: Rhodes Scholar (1905), author of five books, former Director of the School of Slavonic Studies in London, England. He hosted Winter Session students weekly in his small cottage, serving café au lait and stale doughnuts. He insisted on hearing our stories and rarely told his own. He also demanded that we memorize Wordsworth's poem, *Daffodils*:

> I wander'd lonely as a cloud
>   That floats on high o'er vales and hills,
> When all at once I saw a crowd,
>   A host, of golden daffodils...

It was how he prodded us into acknowledging that literature and education were so very important, that the Christian Leadership Training School was an experience of study as much as fun. Uncle Bill amazed all the summer campers when he would take his daily jump into the lake and swim to shore. He would surprise me when, dressed in his red plaid shirt-jacket and blue jeans, he would work with me in the gardens and know the names of all the plants – in Latin!

~ *Jody Dudley*

Jody Dudley was at various times between 1964 and 1972 a Winter Session student, summer and Winter Session staff, full-time grounds/maintenance staff, and board member.

Note: W. J. Rose wrote a history of the Christian Leadership Training School in 1963.

programs & program leadership

Naramata Centre is both part of, and on the edge of, the institution. This position has allowed things to happen here.

~ ALLISON RENNIE, PROGRAM DIRECTOR

Naramata Centre has a tradition of offering innovative ways of teaching and vibrant program topics well in advance of the national United Church, which sometimes elicits raised eyebrows from the "establishment." It is a centre characteristic worth exploring, because understanding how it came to be and why it continues today provides insight into the nature of the centre itself.

The centre's founders and their colleagues were an innovative group. They held a prophetic vision for the Christian Leadership Training School. Their ideals were new to the church at the time and met with some resistance at the national level. Despite this, their collective charisma, persistence, and energy allowed their vision to come to fruition in 1947 with the opening of the school. Over the years, other innovative and creative thinkers (including volunteers, paid leadership staff, program committee and board members) have discovered that Naramata Centre is a place to meet and share ideas and experiences.

Program content has always been influenced by local, national, and world events. The "transitions" theme of 1980 reflected that

> ...we are becoming aware of the reality and significance of living in what has been called "...a worldwide period of transition"...This reality is clearly affecting the many folk with whom we are in contact. Economic issues such as inflation and unemployment; social questions concerning cultural diversity and an increasingly pluralistic society; the growing pressure on the family and community; and the desire of each of us, as individuals, to have control over our lives, are all part of the transition...The general theme which will guide our programming over the next year will be the reality of the transformation taking place, and how we might respond in an informed, realistic, and faithful way.[1]

The centre's international connections also contributed to the development and integration of new classes and programs. Ivan Cumming,[2] and his wife, Nina, were one-time executive members of the Association for Creative Change, an international network of creative, progressive and experiential thinkers. The Cummings formed a British Columbia chapter, which met in Naramata in the 1970s. (See more on Ivan Cumming on p. 88).

Naramata Centre is a member of Oikosnet North America, an ecumenical association of retreat centres.

Membership in other international networks of learning and retreat centres has provided opportunities for multi-cultural learning exchanges. The centre has hosted guests from countries such as Ghana, India, and Central America. Visitors have shared their experiences of the Third World and brought in fresh perspectives in a way that was impossible in the church itself. The centre came to view the world in a new light, and shifted program emphasis accordingly. Ultimately, these international influences provide a platform for the centre's justice orientation.

> *There's a spiritual level at which the centre is held and guided and pushed – I wouldn't want to think that it's all about human work."*
>
> ~ ALLISON RENNIE

The Learning Lab

One of the most dramatic examples of teaching innovation was an educational movement known as "lab learning." Lab, an abbreviation for laboratory, refers to small group learning where participants are encouraged to "experiment" with new behaviours, gather "data" from others in their group, and make choices about their future behaviour based on the feedback. Lab learning originated with the NTL

Institute in Maine in 1947 and was integrated into the centre's programming in the 1960s.

Lynn Maki, Executive Secretary of Alberta and Northwest Conference, remembers the years when the centre was known for the lab program.

That was a big innovation. If a ministry person was having a challenging time or needing to develop inter-personal skills, Presbyteries would often direct them to the Naramata Centre lab programs. The centre was quite famous not just locally, but on the [North American] continent for work done in inter-personal development. That whole lab program was key.

A word about labs and lab sequence from *Good News*, 1978.

A Basic Laboratory in Human Relations focuses on basic learning about human interaction as observed and reflected on from the inside. Participants get in touch with what happens to them personally within a group, and very often become articulate about their feelings, roles, group pressures, personal biases, etc. Learning theories are related to these experiences, or grow out of them. Insights around such issues as conflict management, openness, communications styles, etc. and skills related to these areas are encouraged.

Basic learning about group processes is also an important aspect of basic laboratories. Leadership needs and styles, decision making, group norms, education styles, degrees of openness, and quality of caring become the focus of attention and theory building.

Advanced Labs focus on particular subjects, and take basic laboratory experience for granted. Design skills, conflict utilization, advanced personal growth, consulting skills, and the like assume a capacity for openness, an ability to identify feelings, and a background in behavioural science and other learning associated with the basic group laboratory.

The laboratories make use of the latest research in applied behavioural sciences, and were led by people whose credentials, values, and educational style fit the overall purpose of the Naramata Centre.

Sexual Orientation Policy

One of the most significant examples of being "on the edge" in programming has been Naramata Centre's inclusion of gays and lesbians. By 1982, the centre had a policy on sexual ethics and boundaries for staff. In that same year, the staff asked that the policy be edited to include a statement that sexual orientation would not be a basis for discrimination in hiring. Although their request met with some resistance, staff members persisted, and the personnel committee developed a sexual orientation policy that was approved by the board in 1983. The centre then developed the program *Dialogue on Homosexuality*, and invited equal numbers of gays, lesbians, and heterosexuals to participate. The program was then made available to churches and groups for use in their own settings.

The centre continues to direct its programming into areas where the national church hasn't yet ventured. The annual *Imagine* retreat for gay, lesbian, bi-sexual, and transgendered people provides a warm welcome for individuals who still don't feel safe in their own congregations, or who are not out in their communities, or who are afraid at work.[3]

Naramata Centre's commitment to being a place where the real and relevant issues and questions of life are explored meant it was well placed to provide leadership to the wider church when the church was debating questions of sexuality at its General Council in 1988. The issue of ordaining gays and lesbians came to a head when a sessional committee (chaired by former centre staff member Marion Best) recommended to the United Church General Council that all persons who profess faith in Jesus Christ, regardless of their sexual orientation, be eligible to be members of the United Church; and all members of the church be eligible for the ordered ministry. The recommendation was adopted. Says Best,

> That was something of a breakthrough and also a very tumultuous time in the church. About 20,000 people left overnight, and a lot of ordained people left and went to other churches. It was a painful time, and at the same time, the centre was really firm about their stand. They started holding May weekends that have since become significant for gays and lesbians. One lesbian couple said to me: "There is nowhere else we can go with our little girl and know that we are absolutely welcome"...I think the centre took leadership.

Allison Rennie writes,

> In the 1980s, Naramata Centre was one of the very few places where the church was engaged in meaningful dialogue about sexuality, homosexuality, faith, and life. It was a place that was willing to take risks to align itself with gay and lesbian people, and invite the whole church into the learning. Like many other queer people at that time, I lived part of my life in secret. At church, I hid my human sexuality. In gay and lesbian circles at large, I hid my faith identity. Naramata Centre was a place where this hiding from myself didn't need to happen – as much at least! And now, 20 years later, the United Church of Canada and Canadian society are in such a different place. I know that the risks the centre took to be a place of safety and dialogue contributed to this phenomenal social change. In some ways, it is truly incredible. I am full of gratitude for what courage and faith centre staff lived then so that I can enjoy certain rights and freedoms and responsibilities today.

Other Edges

The centre offers programs that address issues that society may be awake to but not really engaged in. Several summers have included interfaith dialogue opportunities, facilitated by Jewish, Christian, and Muslim leaders. The relaxed, inclusive Naramata environment allowed participants to talk in a neighbourly fashion, rather than at an academic level. The centre has also served as a site for native and non-native teachers and students from residential schools to join in healing circles and learning settings.

One way we've tried to [keep the centre vital] is to offer programs on poverty, Native rights, sexism, nuclear issues, world development, ecology, Bible studies with justice/liberation themes, corporate responsibility, and ethical decision making.

~ GOOD NEWS *JANUARY 1982*

Sometimes, programs "just happen" because relationships develop. One such relationship was created between Naramata Centre and the En'owkin Centre (located on the Penticton Indian Reserve in the Okanagan Nation territory of the Syilx speaking people in British Columbia). The respective executive directors agreed to enter into a partnership without any outcomes, without any plans to do programs or projects together, and with the focus on building a relationship. The no-outcome partnership lasted for about two years; by the third year they had more mutual program involvement than they could manage.

Naramata Centre's community outreach programs for people with mental illness came about through input from Winter Session and summer program participants.

Summer Programs

Kerry Ellison and family, with outdoor fridge, 1974

The centre's summer programs have long been the heart of its public interface. Originally called "vacation courses" and introduced at the centre in 1948, they were a modern version of the "camp meeting," a tradition in Canada going back to the 1800s. The Methodist Church of Canada organized the original very popular and affordable outdoor gatherings, where a temporary village of tents was set up around a preaching area. The camps lasted several days, and provided an opportunity for worship in a social setting. In the 21st century, Naramata Centre's summer programs retain elements of the camp meetings.

Naramata Centre stands apart from other education and retreat centres in the prominence and fullness of its multi-generational summer program. At one time, summer programs were primarily geared to adults. However, a key development in the 1970s was the decision to focus the life of the centre on children and youth as much as on adults. Now, the summer program emphasis is on the wider community experience: worship; intergenerational learning; evening events; high quality programs for children and youth; a schedule that honours the needs of families with young children, and opportunities for youth to socialize.

The first time I came to Naramata I was a toddler. Now ...Intergenerational Week... gives me a chance to do activities with my parents. Naramata is great! It's a place that teaches us to care for each other and our planet!

~ MATT MONTEITH-FORSYTH, AGE 12

Since 1980, the centre has offered summer programming literally for all ages. Before then, parents needed to make their own arrangements for morning childcare with local youths. As a result of persistent promptings from people like board member Gwenneth Foster Newell, and with the active support of staff members Donna and Tim Scorer, the Infants and Toddlers Program began in a small room in the basement of McLaren Hall. The following year (1981), Children's House, a building directly south of the hall, became the permanent location for the program. "As co-ordinator that first summer, I well remember the shock of the first week, with 12 babies, 12 caregivers, and daily rain," recalls Mary Robertson.

Mom, how do they do that at Naramata when they make you feel safe and welcome and good inside, how do they do that?

~ CAMERON FRASER-MONROE, AGE 7

Campground known as Skunk Hollows

"The principle of one-to-one care for each child remains a core value for the program," Robertson adds. "The benefit to parents has also been profound, giving them the freedom to focus on their own learning and personal renewal." She also points out that another exciting benefit has been the development of a fine cadre of young people from Naramata village who have been trained as caregivers over the past 27 years.

The centre also provides a 'buddy' to accompany a child or adult with special needs if required during the summer program.

For a sample of summer programs from the 1960s through to present day, see Appendix B.

For Kerry Ellison,

> Naramata [summer programs] meant FREEDOM. Freedom for my mother to take enriching classes without the worry of childcare; freedom for my father to explore the

Worship at the beach, 1973

geology and fruit offerings of the area through photography, walking, and biking; freedom and safety for us children to try out new ways of being in the world in age-appropriate groupings; freedom to make music; freedom to move our bodies on land and in water. We still consider Naramata Centre our second home, a place of nurture and growth. Another mother.

And it has been happening all over again, as my husband, Kevin McLachlan, and I have brought our son Shane here for the past ten years. It means FREEDOM for the three of us too, although we each have an individual take on that term. Perhaps it could be said that Naramata is a place where each of us finds the freedom to discover and "live into" who we truly are.[4]

Resource leader Craig Henderson and program participants, 2007

Naramata Centre Youth and Youth Ministry Programs

What is it about Naramata Centre that is so valuable for teenagers? According to past board member Marion Taylor, it's Integrity. There's a great deal of integrity among the staff here... If you watch, you see staff here talking to the kids, and the child has their total attention. [Staff members] don't talk down to them. The kids are validated – it is lived out that they are worthwhile as persons. In schools, often... they're not recognized as being people in their own right.

The centre gives children a real boost in the development of their characters and personalities. They learn to value themselves and as they incorporate that, they in turn show that back to the world. At Naramata there's a feeling of acceptance and inclusion.

In 1983, Naramata Centre staff members Marion Best and Sue Laverty set up the Tentmakers Youth Ministry Training Program. Its purpose was to manifest the centre's commitment to equipping principled leaders for the church, and providing young people with leadership skills. Laverty and Best created opportunities for students to learn in day-long or weekend sessions. Ken Mitchell and Walter Wink, among others, taught topics that included caring skills, transformation Bible study, and empathetic and compassionate ministry.

For many students, Tentmakers was a natural progression after Winter Session. The first three months of Tentmakers were held at the centre. Students prepared to lead the summer senior teen program by asking themselves, "How do I relate to a group of people?" and "How can I design, carry out and evaluate programs?" At the end of the summer program, and for the next nine months, the students "interned" in congregations that had volunteered to support them.

Barb McFadyen-Smuin was in the first Tentmaker program, and describes her intern experience at Penticton United Church.

> We worked with youth programs and the intergenerational program, planning to bring the generations together. We had monthly check-ins with our facilitators, Marion Best and Sue Laverty... We would gather at Naramata Centre and spend an extra day or two evaluating what was happening in our home congregation. Then we would go back to the congregation. We did that for nine months, and then we came back to the centre and had the option of working a second summer using the skills we had learned through the year.

Tentmakers ran for about ten years. In 1997 it evolved into the Youth Ministry Certificate Program in B.C. Conference, and the Youth Ministry Diploma Program in Alberta and Northwest Conference.

The Youth Ministry Certificate Program focuses on training people for youth ministry leadership. Sponsored by the B.C. Conference and Naramata Centre, the intensive year-long program is designed for those who see youth ministry as an avocation rather than a vocation. There is no cookie cutter approach to this program. Instead, leaders give considerable attention to drawing out each participant's gifts, skills, and interests, and base their teaching on these. Course enrollment is limited to six people per year.

I know that we are changing the world because of our dedication to listening, honouring, valuing, equipping, and empowering young people.

~ALLISON RENNIE

Also in the arena of youth ministry, Naramata Centre provides pre-event seminars, weekend workshops, and an integration event for people who offer themselves in leadership with children and youth in the church through the Children and Youth Ministry Institute. Music and worship are part of the event. Participants have opportunities to engage with highly qualified resource people in Christian education, and share in worship and singing together.

Doris Kizinna, Conference Minister for Youth and Young Adults, writes,

> Since the beginning of my connection to the centre, Naramata equals for me a cold November weekend when youth from all over British Columbia gather to be the church together. Icy wind off the lake, the great hall alive with the energy and vibrancy of youth, cozy meals in the dining hall, the chapel on a dark winter night filled with song and prayer. Since the early 1980s, Naramata Centre has been home to B.C. Youth Conference, an annual gathering for youth in the United Church where community, learning, inspiration, exploring faith and connection with God are the focus. I went to my first Youth Conference when I was 15 and a whole new world opened up for me. I met leaders who I wanted to be like, I met lifelong friends, and I experienced God's presence.

The Healing Pathway

The Healing Pathway is a program created and offered by Naramata Centre. The pathway trains and mentors individuals who wish to develop their healing gifts and skills within the Christian tradition. The pathway also supports individuals on their spiritual journeys and assists congregations and communities to develop healing ministries.

The Healing Pathway is made up of four phases. The first two are typically held in communities or congregations; the last two are usually held at Naramata Centre. Healing Pathway practise groups are now active in most provinces.

In 1992, after completing Healing Touch instructor training in Colorado, Rochelle Graham wrote to Naramata Centre offering to give a talk about her passion for the work. After her successful presentation, the centre decided to offer Healing Touch programs the next year.

Graham taught the first classes to Winter Session and summer program participants at the centre, and to congregations throughout Alberta and British Columbia. Sunnybrook United Church in Red Deer, Alberta, and volunteers from First United Church in Vancouver pushed to have a unique curriculum developed for the church.

Healing from the heart means to connect to the divine. When we allow the divine to work through us, infinitely more is possible.

ROCHELLE GRAHAM

"After three years of teaching, it became clear that this work was quickly growing, and needed a home. Naramata Centre was the logical location for what was to be named the Healing Pathway," explains Graham.

In 1996, Graham and the centre's management team created the formal Healing Pathway, grounded in the United Church. They formed an advisory team to create values, guidelines, and a code of ethics. Graham talks about setting up the Healing Pathway.

> We agreed that for the program to flourish, it needed the structure and the credibility that Naramata Centre could offer. The centre also provided space to hold workshops in a retreat setting, and the special atmosphere that supported the profound healing work.

> The basic curriculum was the medical/nursing model, which defined the energy in scientific terms. The class participants kept challenging me to redefine the content into Christian theology. At this point, I was the Director of Mission Effectiveness at St. Paul's Hospital in Vancouver. Their mission statement spoke about carrying on the healing mission of Jesus. The work evolved by living the question, "What does it mean to carry on the healing mission of Jesus?"

> I remember the first time I asked class participants to ask God to work through their hands (instead of simply voicing the intent to help). It was as though someone had turned on

one hundred light bulbs in the room. I began to experience the theology of "I am the light of the world." I was continually amazed at how the curriculum was led by God and my job was to listen and respond.

In 1998, the curriculum was reviewed and adopted as the Naramata Centre Healing Pathway. The Healing House (then held in Lyall House) originally opened for two weeks as a pilot project.

"While it is important to honour the Pathway's history in that it developed from the foundation of Healing Touch International, there are many unique aspects about the Pathway, including techniques and how the energy is held," says Julie Gerhardt, Healing Pathway Director since 2007.

Catherine Awai was Director of the Pathway from 2000 to 2007. She was central to the development of this educational program, overseeing instructor training processes, documentation, and ongoing curriculum changes, as well as providing support for community and congregational practice groups. Awai held the vision that Graham had for the Healing Pathway, and it continues to evolve.

Since 2001, about 3,700 people from across Canada have completed at least Phase 1 of the Pathway. At present there are 20 instructors and three instructors-in-training. Growing numbers of training sessions are being offered across Canada.[5]

Naramata Centre has proven to be a place where people come to learn in community. Its programs offer input from leaders, experiential activity, and group discussion. The variety of learning methods enables participants to integrate their experiences into their lives and make a difference in the world long after their program ends.

This nurturing environment also serves the conference groups that use Naramata Centre for their events. Read more about this in Chapter 4.

Program Leadership

Many people have contributed to creating the centre's innovative and exciting programs. The centre honours and thanks its many supporters and friends, including past and present volunteers, program leaders and participants, staff, board members, committee members, Capital Campaign team members, and Naramata village residents.

Four individuals in particular have made unique contributions to the centre and a history would not be complete without recognizing their work. All are honorary members of the Naramata Centre Society.

We had the freedom to try almost anything. You knew there were boundaries, but you could try things that a congregation probably couldn't try. The clergy would really enjoy coming [to the centre].

I remember we offered unemployed people the chance to come to the centre for free programs. They had to get themselves here, but they didn't pay to be here. We offered a couple of years of that in the 1980s, when things were tough.

~ MARION BEST

Marion Best

In 1977, long-time program participants Marion and Jack Best were invited to work in program administration and fundraising at the centre. The Bests also led marriage enrichment programs, and under the auspices of the centre took them to churches and organizations around B.C. After Jack retired in 1980, Marion's position expanded to include program leadership, where she

Jack and Marion Best

put into practice skills she had learned working alongside mentors Ivan Cumming, Elaine Peacock, Roy Wood, and Tom Brown.

Organizing a World Council of Churches event at Naramata was the catalyst for Marion's interest in global issues, and led her to initiate the centre's international program. Marion left her staff position in 1987, but continues to support the centre.

Marion was moderator of the United Church of Canada from 1994 to 1997, and vice-moderator of the World Council of Churches from 1998 to 2006. In 2008, Marion co-chaired the centre's Capital Campaign.

Ivan Cumming

When Ivan Cumming left his position as B.C. Field Secretary for Christian Education to become the director of Naramata Centre in 1968, it marked the beginning of a new direction in the centre's development. The United Church had just introduced its "New Curriculum" for Sunday schools and adult study programs, which was based on a more contemporary style of teaching. At the centre, Cumming – minister, facilitator, educator – introduced new programming and teaching methods that influenced a generation of young people.

Ivan and Nina Cumming

Cumming continued to support the Observation Practise Schools launched by the National Church. People from congregations came to learn the techniques of observing, practicing, and evaluating, and then took these skills back to congregations, mainly for use in Sunday schools. He also introduced lab learning and emphasized the importance of self-awareness and personal relationships. He encouraged people to use their gifts training for leadership. His creativity and skills inspired staff, resource people, and program participants alike.

Cumming led Naramata Centre through a very successful period of change and renewal. He seemed to have his finger on the pulse of society's rapid change and was able to infuse the essence throughout the centre. A quote from a United Church *Observer* article in 1978 captures his understanding of the need to stay current very well. "If you're avant garde and the church catches up, you're not avant garde anymore...The centre should be doing whatever the rest of the church is not doing.[6]

Following a World Council of Churches meeting held at Naramata Centre in 1981, Ivan and his wife, Nina, were invited to give leadership in Trinidad for five months. Cumming left the centre and for the next six years served as executive secretary for B.C. Conference. In 1987, he joined Nina on the pastoral team of Ryerson United Church in Vancouver.

When Cumming passed away in 2007, he left a legacy of 60 years of ministry in the United Church of Canada. Nina Cumming is an honorary member of the Naramata Centre Society.

Sue Laverty

Sue Laverty

Sue Laverty was on staff at the centre from 1981 to 1990. An ordained Baptist minister from the liberal stream predominant at the Acadia Divinity School in Nova Scotia where she studied, she had a loving appreciation of scripture and a deep social conscience. Her prayers were extemporaneous, from the heart, funny, and disturbing to the status quo. She often ended her commissioning and benediction with "God help us if we do, and God help us if we don't."

Laverty's passion was working with children and youth. She respected them for who they were and what they embodied. Her playfulness, energy, and love brought out the best in children and the people she taught. Because of her firm commitment to the children's ministry, Laverty insisted that young adults working with children be extensively trained and supervised, and also adequately compensated for their work. Those principals are her legacy. Laverty contributed positively to the lives of hundreds of young people. Her partner, dori petty[7], also offered leadership for children's programs and later was one of the co-ordinators of the Children's House.

Go forth and do the next right thing.

~ *Sue Laverty paraphrasing Holocaust survivor and Nobel Laureate Elie Wiesel*

When Laverty died unexpectedly in 1994, dozens of those she had mentored and encouraged attended a memorial service at the Naramata Centre beach. Her puppets, well-worn Bible, pottery, and music were displayed on a table as reminders of her many gifts.

dori petty coordinating juniors in the summer program *Under the Sky* in the late 1980s

Tim and Donna Scorer

Tim Scorer

Tim Scorer is a freelance educator, writer, editor, and spiritual director. His association with the centre began in 1979 when he was invited to lead Winter Session. His work as leader and educator (as part of the program staff and management team) covered a broad spectrum of activities. He created summer programs, introduced summer staff to experiential learning, led early morning worship at the beach, facilitated daily meetings of the resource people, cracked through long agendas at management meetings, and spent time as Program coordinator with Mary Jo Leddy, Joyce Rupp, Walter Wink, and others. Scorer writes,

I still remember in my early years at the centre sitting in groups as a co-leader with skilled and gifted educational facilitators like Elaine Peacock, Linda Green, Catherine Ross, Marion Best, and Ivan Cumming, and being in awe of their capacity to facilitate learning based on the "here and now" experience of people in a group. I had come from a background in traditional high school classroom teaching; and seeing what was possible in transforming people's lives through experiential teaching was an incredible eye opener. It seemed like a skill way beyond my capacity to achieve and yet, here I am now looking back over the years of involvement in centre life and appreciating that I, too, could be transformed through the power of skillfully led experiential learning processes. The highlights of my involvement with the centre are all the moments along that journey of learning.

Still very much involved with the centre as a resource person, Scorer is leader of the second Common Life program, in which ten people meet in community for six weekends over two years to develop Christian spiritual practices. His partner, Donna Scorer, started the Children's House in 1980 and had served as program resource for children and youth summer programs.

Don McKay

*N*ative *Elders have been telling me for quite some time now
that the sacred and healing places of our ancestors are still
there; all you have to do is look for them.*

*Over the years I have begun to see Naramata Centre with new
(old) eyes. For me, this place is sacred, healing, and magical.*

*I remember hearing about Naramata many years ago...
Back then, Naramata was this mysterious place where smart
people went to get smarter. Back then it was a place I was afraid
of, because I lived in fear.*

*In the late 1990s, I presented workshops on residential schools
throughout the province. Our local United Church minister
suggested that a workshop at Naramata would be a good idea. I
was a bit reluctant, but agreed to be one of the presenters.*

*Since then, Naramata has become the place that I go to in
order to get recharged. I look forward to my times at Naramata
because there is community and solitude, depending on what I
need, and because there I am treated as an equal.*

I have often said that the world needs more Naramatas.

*Naramata has helped transform me. It was there that I began
to find my true self. I also learned how to take bits of Naramata
and transplant them at home.*

*I feel sad when I leave that place, but I am very glad it exists.
Naramata is, for me, a Garden of Eden.*

~ WII HAUGHTKM SKIIK (DON M. McKAY) IS A MEMBER OF THE TSIMSHIAN NATION
LOCATED ON THE NORTHWESTERN COAST OF BRITISH COLUMBIA.

chapter 4

a place to come home to

Staff give more of themselves because it is a special place to work, and because it gives so much to other people. One of the delights for me was to see people arrive at the centre just worn out and tired, and then leave buoyant and happy and bouncing.

~ JUDY (FORMO) BATEMAN, FORMER OFFICE STAFF MEMBER AND OFFICE SUPERVISOR FOR 32 YEARS

The 23 acres that make up Naramata Centre are serene and beckoning. The sandy beach, the cherry orchard, the whisper of stately willows, the call of the quail, the scent of sage in the dry desert air, the burble of Naramata Creek are all virtually unchanged since the centre opened in 1947. However, the facilities have gone from a hostel with one sink and classes in the village church basement to the comprehensive retreat centre it is today.

The Development of the Site

1948   The officers' quarters and mess hall buildings from the Canadian Forces Base in Vernon, British Columbia, were purchased and moved to Naramata to create McLaren Hall.

View of Orchard Court in the early days

1950   First cottage units, Cottage Court, built.

1951   Beach property acquired and the principal's house built.

1952   Beach fireplace and playground built.

1953   Second staff house built on the corner of First and Gwendolyn.

1954   Robson House (now Children's House) acquired and East Court built.

1955   Dock and the first camping area built; more property acquired. Total holdings now about 12 acres.

1956   More property purchased and Orchard Court built.

1958   Lyall House and Cuthbert House acquired.

1959   Sutton House remodelled.

1961   Columbia Hall opened. Site now consists of 17 acres with 150 yards of lake frontage.[1]

East Court in 1959

1962	Cuthbert House moved and new staff house built at Third and Gwendolyn.	1999	Chalmers Chapel opened.
		2000	Labryinth added.
1963	Alberta Hall completed.	2002	The Healing House created.
1972-83	McLaren Hall continuously under renovation, transformed from dormitories to classrooms, offices, and craft facilities.	2003	Sacred Garden established.
		2005	Land sold to Naramata Seniors Housing Society.
1979	Maple Court opened	2008	Orchard Court demolished and two new Orchard Court buildings begun.

...the idea of the bedroom doors opening into the lounge [Maple Court] came about. It's not a bunch of individuals here. People are here to be in community.

~ MARION BEST

When the centre opened in 1947, a supply of drinking water was available from three dams in the hills above Naramata.

Beginning in the mid-1980s, health authorities declared the water unfit to drink and at various times issued "boil water" advisories. This meant that for some years the centre had to provide bottled water for its guests at a cost of $12,000 a year. A new water treatment plant situated above and southeast of the centre opened in 2007 and Naramata Centre now gets its water from there. The water for the plant comes from intakes deep in Lake Okanagan.

Almost every building at the centre has its own septic tank and there are two main septic fields. One large field is located in the ball field behind East Court and serves all of the buildings that are west of Columbia Hall. Wastewater from Columbia Hall and all buildings east of it flows by gravity to collection tanks behind Alberta Hall, settles there, and then flows by gravity to the second disposal field located below the chapel.

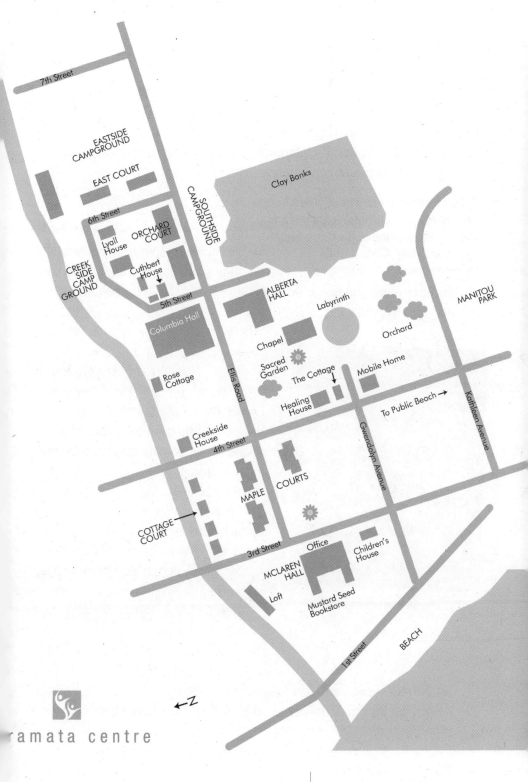

Naramata Grounds in 2008

Setting the Stage for the Next 50 Years

In 2007, the board approved a Master Site Plan that outlined the centre's future plans. The plan was prepared by architects Greg Johnson and Craig Burns in consultation with community members, summer program leaders, program participants, and staff. It sets the vision for the next 50 years, includes a list of suggested projects, renovations, and upgradings, and considers environmental issues such as those associated with sewer systems and the riparian zone.

A place of spirit? Over the years, ghosts have been reportedly seen in the Children's House, Cottage Court Number 7, and Alberta Hall.

"There isn't any intention to increase the capacity of the centre," says Diane Ransom, Director of Development. "We have an optimal community size, especially in the summer time. We have a commitment to maintain green space, to be sustainable, and to integrate buildings and landscape with the surrounding Okanagan."

The $3 million Capital Campaign, launched in 2006, will restore and refresh the centre and create its future.

The goals of the campaign are to create:

Diane Ransom

- Comfortable, fully accessible accommodation
- Welcoming, accessible, and up-to-date program facilities
- Nurturing and efficient hospitality services
- An environmentally responsible "green" Naramata Centre

A Poem for Staff at Naramata Centre

Hospitality is of the body.
It's a certain movement of the muscle.

A focusing of the eye

(I see you,
there, in that space beside the peach tree.
I notice.)

A twitching of the skin near the mouth – ¾ of a smile

(And it's pleasant
seeing you there,
in the shade of the tree.)

Sometimes, hospitality is the clicking of the tongue
against the teeth and the roof of the mouth.

(Hello.
How's it going.
Are you still here?)

Or an arcing of the arm to let you in.

Hospitality's the lifting of the arms to carry things

(clean towels
soap
a roll of toilet paper)

keeping things straight, making a job easier for others,

Or a swing of the wrist and hand to clean things up

(a mirror
a sink
a floor)

"We like things nice for those who come,"
says the woman with the blonde and curly hair.

Hospitality is the bending of a body by a rose bush

(digging
clipping)

"I enjoy it," the man in the straw hat says,
"helping things grow,
making the place attractive for those who come."

It's a manipulation of the fingers in order to fix things

(a knob
a lamp
a broken faucet)

Then standing tall.
Hospitality's wearing a feather in your hat – and red socks.

Hospitality is carrying a timer in
  the pocket of your smock.

("I've Yorkshire pudding in the oven.
The timing's tricky,"
says the young man with the
  smooth brown hair.)

Hospitality is physical, not spiritual or intellectual.

And yet, without the spirit
the body's movements are pale and sickly.

Hospitality is not always noticed.

(Except by some.
Angels always notice.
And God, of course.)

But if hospitality isn't there,
everything else is worth nothing –
throw it out with dead and rotting things.

You can't always do anything with hospitality.
Except let it be.
And say thanks.

~ *GLORIA SAWAI* [2]

The Centre's Staff

Naramata Centre can say it truly specializes in hospitality! Sixty years worth of thank-you cards, letters of appreciation, personal words of gratitude and donations attest to that. Credit must go in large part to the centre's staff, who have a history of "going the extra mile."

Dirk van Battum, the centre's Cleaning Services Department Supervisor, speaks to the task of making guests welcome.

Naramata Centre is not just a place to visit or have a meeting, it is an experience. We work to create an environment where our guests can create, refresh, and renew. In so doing, we strive to give our guests memories of not just a nice warm inviting place but of an experience that played a part in their future direction in life.

We help late arrivals find their keys and accommodations, and do anything else it takes to make our guests comfortable, from unplugging toilets to getting extra bedding or adjusting the heat in rooms. Our goal is to meet the needs of the guest. This means not just preparing the meeting rooms and accommodations, but making the entire stay a pleasant one. The challenge is to meet the needs of a variety of people with the resources available.

The centre's support of its staff, in both their professional and personal lives, continues to be a hallmark of its workplace ethics. For example, the centre changed the position of summer staff co-ordinator to that of summer staff chaplain in order to better support the 30 or so young people who live together in Alberta Hall and work in community as summer staff every year.

It's about... providing a space for you to grow yourself as staff – for the staff to take on for themselves things that are struggles in everyday life.

~ GRAHAM BROWNMILLER, CHAPLAIN, 2008

Office staff help to create a special welcome for guests, 2008
l to r: Kathy Dean, Shana Miller, Wendy Gowe, Karen Moore

For some of them, it may be their first time away from home, or perhaps they have just graduated from high school or finished their first year of university. The chaplain lends an ear and provides guidance on many subjects, helping them resolve conflicts with room-mates, increase their leadership confidence, and explore questions about faith and spirituality.

For summer staff member Po Yi Liu, the centre's support was both surprising and appreciated: "I never knew how much work, thought, and preparation is put into making the summer staff feel comfortable."

Summer Coordinators, 2000

In the 1990s, some issues around working conditions prompted staff members to investigate the possibility of unionizing. They met with a representative from the Canadian Union of Public Employees (CUPE), and later voted nearly 100 per cent in favour of joining. On May 26, 1994, the Naramata Centre board received notice of the decision of the B.C. Labour Relations Board to grant certification to CUPE Local 608 for employees of the Naramata Centre Society.

**CUPE
LOCAL 608**

Jim Ellis, a board member who led negotiations on behalf of the centre, writes,

> This decision, while no surprise, created anxiety, fear, excitement, and, for some staff, joy. Whoever heard of a United Church organization with union employees? Was this a threat to our values, our financial well-being, our ability to provide meaningful programs? Or was this a way to address some employment issues within the organization? We were about to find out.
>
> The two sides appointed representatives for the upcoming collective agreement negotiations. At the first meeting on August 17, 1994, we began the difficult process of working out a collective agreement... in May 1995, we signed off on the first Naramata collective agreement.
>
> At the end of the work on the agreement, the two teams were working together in harmony and with a shared vision of how this partnership could and would be played out. The agreement would result in a stronger, more trusting staff relationship and the history of the centre shows the partnership forged in that time of fire has been successful.

...our working relationships and environment are characterized by mutual respect, collegiality, and genuine concern for the centre's ministry.

~ MARY ROBERTSON

Former Directors John and Mary Robertson

Sabbaticals

Sabbaticals offer another way for centre staff to be supported. Opportunities for management staff to take sabbaticals have nourished not only the individual but also indirectly affected the centre's programming and relationships with the wider world. Tim Scorer, who served on the centre's management team for 24 years, describes how his sabbaticals made a difference.

> ... in 1982, our three children went to school in Newcastle in northeast England, while I went to the University of Newcastle to study drama in education with Dorothy Heathcote, an international leader in that field. It wasn't at all clear to me what the application of that learning was to the program work I was doing at Naramata Centre; however, as the years passed I realized how profoundly I had been affected by that experience, and I started to be able to identify the specific impact of that time in things as diverse as worship planning, leadership, experiential learning design, and leadership for organizational development.
>
> Then, in 1988, [my wife] Donna and I decided to be even more adventurous in our shared family learning. The five of us took our back packs and trekked around India, Indonesia, Thailand, and Malaysia for six months. We presented this to the centre as a family sabbatical by which we hoped to encourage other families to consider taking time out together to do something that would contribute to the learning of all. Obviously, it might not be something as ambitious as a six month international trek, but the same philosophy and principles might apply. For me, as a centre staff person, the international experience was a source of great insight and opening. It led me to be more actively involved with the global network of centres and particularly with the World Council of Churches courses for leadership in lay training.

Hosting

Naramata Centre continues to be a desirable place to hold meetings for hundreds of congregations and groups. Many return year after year. Some notable past and present regulars include the Sal'i'shan Native Training Institute, quilting groups, BC 4-H, the Blossom Tours, the Family Support Institute, CUPE, and the congregations of Canadian Memorial and Notre Dame churches.

In the mid-1980s, the centre took on a major promotion to increase use of its facilities by hosted groups. Letters and a new brochure were sent to 150 existing and potential client groups across British Columbia and Alberta. Inquiries started to roll in, including one from a B.C. First Nations group that made its first booking in 1988.

Recalls Dave Perry, a former centre program host:

I remember them well. They arrived all day and night by air, car, bus. The kitchen staff had no idea how many to prepare for, but left bag lunches at 10 p.m. for the ones still to come. I stayed up to greet them, guide them to accommodation, and tell them when and where breakfast would be available, and where they were to gather for the opening ceremony and welcome. Next morning, I welcomed them to Naramata Centre, answered questions, and at their invitation participated in the ceremony – a very special and spiritual experience.

Known as the Sal'i'shan Institute, this group met for weeks at a time in the fall and spring over the next ten years. Founded by social worker and educator Bill Mussell (a SKWAH band member and part of the Sto: lo tribe in British Columbia), and funded by Health Canada, Sal'i'shan's purpose was to equip First Nations students with skills to work as practitioners primarily in health, education, and social development in their communities.

More than 1,000 First Nations people graduated from the institute. When funding arrangements changed in the late 1990s, Sal'i'shan's programs at Naramata Centre came to an end. The last programs were held in 2000. Sal'i'shan still exists, but today offers custom-designed programs and focuses on research.

The Canadian Union of Public Employees was also a notable regular at the centre. Linda Sherwood, CUPE social convenor, writes,

> ...Each year, I looked forward to arriving at the centre. On my short drive from Summerland I would feel the stresses of preparing for...our group [visit] slip away. I was heading towards one of my favourite places and about to experience one of my favourite times of the year – the reunion not only with my CUPE family, but with my Naramata family as well.

The World Comes to Naramata

The centre was the meeting site of a World Council of Churches Committee-sponsored conference in October 1977. Thirty-five participants came from lay centres in Asia, Africa, Europe, and the two Americas. Each day a case study describing the relationship of the Bible to the social, political, and cultural situations in a country from one of the six continents was chosen. It was a dramatic time at the centre during which a call brought the sad news that the South African government had banned three black newspapers and 18 anti-apartheid organizations, all known to the delegates.

"We doubt if any group of Christians ever had a more searing, and, at the same time, inspiring experience or a greater opportunity to show their love for one another," concluded a 1977 *Good News* article.

And Naramata Goes Out into the World

Marion Best organized the World Council of Churches gathering at Naramata in 1977, and as a result, spent a sabbatical in Africa and subsequently ended up on the Council's governing body where she was the vice-moderator until 2006. "The centre opened the door of the wider world to me in a way that I don't think would have ever happened for me," says Best.

Special Needs

Naramata Centre also does a stellar job accommodating people with special needs. Berta and Lawrie Fisher tell the story of their son Kevin, who was born with Down Syndrome.

We first went to Naramata for two weeks of the summer program in 1974, when Kevin was 14. We attended every summer after that until Kevin died in the winter of 2001.

Jean Tollefson was the person who encouraged us to go, and in 1974 worked with the board and staff to convince them that the time had come to enlarge the summer program to include children, youth, and adults with developmental challenges. The staff responded enthusiastically. Our contribution to the program was sharing our Naramata experiences with parents in similar situations back in Calgary, and having some of them come to Naramata,

usually for a summer week. Berta was asked one year to come to the centre during summer staff training to share how rewarding living and working with young people with developmental challenges could be.

As parents we watched Kevin grow in confidence as he began to feel safe and secure anywhere on the Naramata campus. One week he would be with one of us in a morning course and the second week he would be with the other. Often the courses would be active ones: music, working with clay, drumming, bird watching. In the afternoons he would listen to music tapes and CDs and later go swimming. He was an enthusiastic swimmer, often swimming under water to retrieve a tennis ball he had tossed a short distance away. In later years he attended the Friday dance on his own, dancing solo or joined by a girl or two who over the years had come to know and understand him. This acceptance by his peers meant a great deal to him and gave him a sense of his own worth.

A glance at the annual catalogue of summer program shows the extent to which people with special needs (more broadly defined as the years go by) are welcomed and accommodated every summer... Naramata is the place to go.

Naramata Centre introduced its "buddy system," which offers support for those with special needs, in 1989. The centre offers financial assistance, in the form of the Heartwood Bursary, to pay a "buddy's" wages for a week.

The Heartwood Bursary

The Heartwood Bursary was created in 1987 with donations from individuals who wished to express their gratitude for the work of Naramata Centre on the occasion of its 40th anniversary. It is also funded by special memorial gifts made in honour of Sue Laverty, Bob McLaren, Kathlene Yetman, and Kathleen Bailey. Fund allocation priorities include low-income young adults and families with young children; low-income persons in distant or remote locations; and persons with disabilities, or their caregivers. The Heartwood Bursary continues to welcome contributions and bequests. Application forms are available on the centre's website www.naramatacentre.net. Anyone in need is encouraged to apply.

Gunnar Tjener

When I arrived in October 1964, Gunnar Tjener was the "maintenance man." A remarkable self-taught Danish immigrant, Gunnar took tender loving care of the centre's facilities for several years. He was creative and innovative. He kept the old bus going (a cast-off B.C. Electric bus that Bob McLaren "scrounged" to use as transportation at the centre) and he converted the McLaren Hall coal furnace to oil in 1964, much to the relief of all the students who had been shovelling coal throughout the winter. Improvements and renovations were made without blueprints! When we added the bathrooms to the end of the Orchard Court cabins, he had the plumbing design sketched out with chalk on the cement floor of the craft shop. He fabricated the underground plumbing there, then took the assembled pipes and laid them into place in the new foundation of the cabins.

Jody Dudley

JODY DUDLEY WAS AT VARIOUS TIMES BETWEEN 1964 AND 1972 WINTER SESSION STUDENT,
SUMMER AND WINTER SESSION STAFF, FULL-TIME GROUNDS/MAINTENANCE STAFF,
AND BOARD MEMBER.

mind, body & spirit

Naramata Centre was a mystery to me when I first arrived in B.C. Indeed, so was the whole Okanagan valley, with its sudden dry sage landscape, trees dipping with ripe fruit and sun glistening golden on the lake. How does a place become known as "holy ground"? Simply because so many have worshipped there and left the imprint of their prayerful yearnings? Or are we drawn to a place because the very hills, water and sky are charged with the presence of creation's connectedness? I wonder about this more every year.

~ Linnea Good

From the time it welcomed its first students in 1947, and continuing to the present, Naramata Centre nourishes and supports the whole person – mind, body, and spirit. Here is a look at some key accomplishments along that journey.

Mustard Seed Bookstore

Irene Hart remembers the summer of 1984 when she set up book displays in the McLaren Hall lounge on Wednesday afternoons. "I wanted to show Naramata Centre staff the possibilities of having more resources available. People that summer had expressed appreciation for the opportunity to get the books the United Church was recommending."

She and Janet Stobie had a vision of a bookstore that would support the centre's courses. "I am not sure where I got such confidence since I had absolutely no bookstore experience or training," recalls Stobie. "Hugh Creighton (a 1984 board member) was essential in making this project work, because as an accountant he understood the need for both me as the manager, and the centre as the risk taker, to make the bookstore financially viable."

In 1985 the Mustard Seed Bookstore opened under Stobie's management. The bookstore name relates to the parable of the mustard seed, a tiny seed full of potential. It also inspired the use of bright yellow paint for the store. "There may have been some trepidation around the colour when the walls were first covered," says Stobie. "But the colour proved to be a good background for the displays and, of course, once dori petty's[1] wonderful mustard seed mural went up on one wall, the room came to life!"

Barb McFadyen-Smuin took over as bookstore manager in 1989. In 1991, she orchestrated a major growth spurt by providing a book display for a large international conference hosted at Naramata Centre. She also began to co-ordinate book displays for congregations, and sold books at various United Church general meetings.

The bookstore was renovated in 2000 and the inventory computerized the following year. Special software enables the bookstore to track what customers buy. In deciding what books to stock, McFadyen-Smuin eagerly combs through publishers' catalogues and considers recommendations from program resource leaders and customers.

Ministry of resources is how I describe it.

~Barb McFadyen-Smuin

Says McFadyen-Smuin,

> It's much more than just selling books. It's about matching people to the resources that will support them... And yes, it's nice to make a sale, but it's more satisfying to hear somebody talk about what they're looking for and then for me to pull things off the shelf and say "this ties in with what you're talking about" and then have them look through the resources to figure it out for themselves. It does feel like a ministry.

The Sacred Garden

The idea for a sacred garden originated in 2002, when Diane Ransom (then the centre's director of operations) and Gwen Steele, a gardener and former nursery owner, were walking through a vacant lot between Chalmers Chapel and the Healing House. Along with the labyrinth, this area had evolved to become the sacred core of the centre, and the addition of a garden as a place for reflection, prayer, and healing seemed to fit.

A small group of avid gardeners joined Ransom and Steele to begin planning and dreaming. Sue Bannerman, a healing touch practitioner, contributed her skills in working with the energetic qualities of place and plants. Jane Ritchie, also a healing practitioner, offered her design talents. Horticulturalist Joanna Clark was expert in creating healing gardens and traditional plant gardens. The group developed a concept that featured seven areas of focus. "We came up with the idea of having seven areas of colours designed to evoke seven different kinds of experiences in the garden," recalls Ransom.

Peace	*White*
Abundance	*Purple*
Healing	*Blue*
Sanctuary	*Green*
Inspiration	*Yellow*
Communion	*Orange*
Love	*Red*

In summer 2003, nine enthusiastic participants signed up for the Build a Sacred Garden program. They began each day with a prayer or reading about gardening, then set to work. Together they raked and sculpted the beds, set in place about 300 feet of pathway edging and moved tons of rocks. Everything was ready by fall, when the Friends of the Sacred Garden planted the garden with drought tolerant plants that would provide colour through the seasons.

There are more than 70 species of trees and shrubs around Naramata Centre's beautiful grounds.

Chalmers Chapel

A simple quiet place... for all people who are open to the presence of spirit to find sanctuary, renewal, and recreation, alone or in community.

~ JIM TAGGART

Located at the base of a clay bank, the chapel is close to the physical heart of the centre and symbolizes the confluence of the centre's ideologies

In the early 1990s, Chalmers United Church in Vancouver disbanded, sold the building, and presented Naramata Centre Society with a cheque for $450,000. It was the congregation's wish that the centre use the money to build a chapel and support programs in leadership development. But not everyone thought a chapel was necessary. "They believed the whole site *was* a chapel and sacred space, and the centre didn't need a dedicated building to worship in," notes Diane Ransom, Director of Development. However, the decision to build was made, and Penticton architect Isabel Chen was engaged to work on the project in conjunction with a committee chaired by Catherine Awai. Says Chen,

> What was really clear from the committee... was honouring the gift and the site. They thought of the entire site as being sacred. We joked about this over the years: we would have weekends where we met and we never talked about the building... We talked about what is Christianity, what is spirituality, and how that is expressed.

> The committee wanted a building that said *welcome.* They also wanted a building that allowed 20 people to join hands together in a circle, and that everyone would feel comfortable in spiritually, but wanted Christian symbols deeply embedded in the building... They wanted natural and native elements incorporated.

A rectangular prism from south to north in both plan and section – representing arms outreached, soaring both southwards and upwards to the sky.

~ JIM TAGGART

Seven sites were considered and the process to choose one took months. Physical constraints included a clay bank to the east, a roadway and lot lines to the west, a drop-off to the south, and magnificent trees to the north.

Former staff and committee member Darryl Auten tells the poignant story of a First Nations elder who was at the centre attending a Sal'i'shan training program in leadership development. The elder was upset because a machine was disturbing the ground where "the quiet place" was to be built and wanted to know what was going on. Says Auten, "They told him that a chapel was to be built, and he said 'Oh, oh, okay. I have walked these grounds every time I come here, and for me and in my tradition, that is the holiest spot on the site.' So whatever intuition we had was affirmed by him."

Local builder Rick Grandbois executed the design, which involved working with massive reclaimed Douglas-fir timbers for the roof structure. The huge 40-foot old-growth beams extend from the narrow north wall and are supported by four groups of four timber posts, each meant to symbolize the four gospels, the four elements, the four seasons, or the four cardinal directions.

The "hand-holding circle" passes between the column clusters, and two other circles are inscribed in the floor. Their intersections are evocative of the fish/piscine/ixthus symbols, which represent Christ in the Christian community, and are also symbols of plenty for both the Christian and First Nations communities.

When the chapel was officially opened in 1999, several former congregation members from Chalmers United Church attended the dedication weekend. Guests walked along a specially designed pathway (a kind of cascading fantail) that guided them into the chapel. This inviting sanctuary, with its views of the lake, was a dream at last achieved. And there was an unexpected bonus. The chapel's acoustical qualities not only beckon the voice to be still, but also prove powerfully evocative during songs of celebration!

The Labyrinth

U sed for centuries in traditions around the world, the labyrinth is a tool for contemplation, prayer, ritual, healing, and personal and spiritual growth. Unlike a maze, a labyrinth has only one path, leading always to the centre.

The Naramata Centre labyrinth, built by Gil and Wilma Giesbrecht in 2000, is a replica of the one laid in the floor of Chartres Cathedral in France in 1220. Using their garden tractor adapted with a specially made front end loader, and a hopper to distribute the gravel, they completed the 65-foot labyrinth in less than three days. Wilma recalls,

Children are often fascinated by the labyrinth and explore it in prayer, or in gleeful running!

At Christmas 1999, we gave ourselves a labyrinth workshop in Red Deer, Alberta. Gil understood the sacred geometry and began making labyrinths in the snow and in the field at home... As God would have it, a very old house burned down just below the chapel at the centre... We said we would love to build a labyrinth... We loaded the truck and a trailer, and we were off... It occurred to us that we had indeed been called and guided to this work with the labyrinth so that the centre could at last have this addition to the sacredness of this place...

There is no "right" way to walk the labyrinth. You might choose to ask a question; repeat a mantra, phrase, or prayer; or simply allow the labyrinth to take you into a meditative state as you walk. The mysterious path that takes us to the centre becomes a metaphor for our own spiritual journey. Going in, we release the cares and concerns that distract us from our Source. The centre of the labyrinth is a place of prayer and meditation where we receive clarity about our lives. As we walk out on the same path that brought us in, we take to community what we have received.

Notice what happens as you walk. Listen to your thoughts as you travel the path.

The Healing House

The Healing House, just west of the chapel, provides a setting for receiving healing from trained practitioners.

People can experience the benefits of Healing Pathway sessions provided by advanced practitioners who come from across Canada and work under the guidance of a mentor.[2] These are rich experiences for both practitioners and individuals receiving treatment.

A Healing Pathway treatment works with the energy of the body. The practitioner's intention is to be an instrument of God's healing power in order to support physical, emotional, and spiritual well-being and wholeness. Specific techniques support the body's ability to heal. Light touch

> Thank you for an experience of the sacred... I feel a living expression of spirit within my heart.

may be used or the practitioners may work with their hands around the body without touching. There may be dialogue or you may receive treatment in silence. (See p. 83 for more about the Healing Pathway.)

The first Healing House was in the former Lyall House, located in the camping area next to Orchard Court and East Court. In 2002 the Blue House was renovated and became the dedicated Healing House. It's now painted red.

Food, Glorious Food!

Naramata Centre is renowned for its delicious, varied, fresh, plentiful, and wholesome food. This quality food may seem to appear magically from the kitchen, but is really the result of careful planning and innovation by professionals who go the extra mile for guests. Food Services Supervisor Colin Drought plans the menus, and along with other staff creates the centre's own recipes. Sometimes he'll test out recipes that have been recommended by a guest. If they are affordable, tasty, and easy to prepare, they could become part of the next year's menus.[3]

> The problem with food is I like it...even more when someone else does the cooking. My hips thank you.

To keep up with current likes and dislikes, he reads every evaluation form – more than 500 in 2008. "We take a close look at everything," he says. "It isn't 1947 anymore. So things change, people change, ideas change."

> Naramata Centre's famous and delicious granola is legendary. Every year, the kitchen goes through 2,000 pounds, and in the summer of 2008 sold 500 one-pound bags!

Drought and his staff pride themselves on being able to cater to special dietary needs. "We tailor-make meals if we have to. It can be difficult at times, but the response forms show that people are ecstatic." Adds Drought, "We try to be middle of the road... Not too spicy, not too mild. Quality is number one."

Thank you to all the kitchen staff for the wonderful food (even without wheat or dairy!). It is obvious how hard you guys work!

~ COMMENT ON EVALUATION FORM

It wasn't always so organized! Sarah Bartner (now Sarah Morgan) came to Naramata from Alberta, volunteered to cook for a week or two, and ended up running the kitchen from January to May 1948 – without pay. Says Bartner,

Sarah Bartner, first cook at the school

> I had not done any major cooking. What I did know, I had seen my mother do...I went into town and bought a cheap pocket cookbook, which was very practical and down to earth...When I look back, I think it was absolutely crazy for someone just out of school to take this on. I really thought when I made the offer that we would go like that for a week and then he [Principal Bob McLaren] would get a cook, but he was the type of fellow that once somebody picked up the shovel, he didn't look back...

Bartner cooked three meals a day, seven days a week, for five months. She used her administrative talents to assemble crews of students to peel potatoes, make the salads, set the table, and do the dishes. "I thought if we ran it like a church camp, with fag duty,[4] we could swing it."

Kitchen duty

Bartner was a one-woman band. At least the menus were easy to plan – they were the same each week. A bread truck that made regular deliveries to Naramata brought groceries. For other items, Bartner drove to Penticton two or three times a week towing a trailer behind the McLarens' 1947 Plymouth.

There was no refrigeration. "I would get the butcher to freeze what I wanted. What I would pick up for tonight's supper would be thawed out, but for the next two suppers it would be frozen...They lined a cupboard to give it a little bit of insulation, and the frozen meat helped to keep the other stuff," Bartner recalls.

Clara Waddell was the first paid cook. "When she [Waddell] took over from me in fall 1948, I made sure she had one day a week off... I would get other students to give her a break... she needed time to breathe. There were times you'd flop into bed and get four hours sleep. Even though I was young and foolish, I knew that wasn't right," adds Bartner.

In the fall of 1948, the kitchen moved from the hostel into a roof-less McLaren Hall. "I remember putting tarps on the roof support if it looked like it was going to rain. If I was making a big pot of soup or stew, I had to keep it covered so the sawdust from the work above wouldn't fall into it," says Bartner.

Chris Grauer, who started work in the kitchen in Columbia Hall in 1968, recalls,

> It was hot – we had no air conditioning. The summers were pretty fierce. And back then, the summer programs went from Saturday night to the next Saturday morning, so there was no free day for the kitchen staff.
>
> We had an old dishwasher. There were no controls on it – you'd turn it on, and it would heat the water until it was at a rolling boil... It was like a steam laundry in there.

Cook Chris Grauer in the early 1970s

THE APPLE DUMPLING GANG

Food services staff, early 1990s
back row, l to r: Colin Drought, Chris Grauer, Jodi Johnston, Jennifer Johnston
front row, l to r: Norm Lepitre, Connie Morrison, Lina Matias, Mija Dicken

As a cook trainee, and as head cook from 1974–1994, Grauer discovered that getting enough staff to cover large events was a challenge. Over the years, the centre has hired many local young people (including high school students) to work in the kitchen. Under the supervision of experienced cooks, they've had the opportunity to learn how to prepare and serve food, and work hard.

> A chicken breast dinner typically calls for 250 chicken breasts, 25 pounds of rice or 50 pounds of potatoes, 35 pounds of each kind of vegetable, plus dessert and fruit.

Money for new equipment has always been scarce, but in 1994 the kitchen received its first new major equipment since the 1960s, with the purchase of two convection gas ovens, a new large mixer, and replacement pots and pans. The dining room was renovated with paint, curtains, carpet, entrance doors, 21 round tables, and 200 burgundy chairs. In 2007, a new steamer was purchased; food is cooked in less time and retains more nutrients.

For many years, food was dished up into large serving bowls, and a "gopher" would take the bowls from the kitchen out to the tables where people ate family style. But that system resulted in a lot of food waste. Today, food is most often served cafeteria style. The problem of what to do with leftovers was resolved in the 1980s, when staff started to package them in freezable containers. "If we have planned on 40 people for dinner, and six or seven people don't show up, we'll package up that exact plate into the container and freeze it within half an hour," explains Drought.

The place offers things that other places don't. And that's the biggest reason I like working here. There's always something new and different.

~ COLIN DROUGHT

The wonderful tradition known as "the smorg" got its start at the centre in the 1970s. It's an event

Kitchen summer staff produced 650 meals a day in 2008!

not to be missed! Not only is the food delicious, but the kitchen staff pull out all the stops to make sure the end-of-the-week feast is visually spectacular too.

In the smorg's early days, cook Lina Taveras would bring in buckets of grapevines and herbs from her own garden, and use her artistic flair to transform the dining room and buffet tables into eye candy. Norm Lepitre (Head Cook from 1994–2005) used his carving talents to magically turn food like olives, celery, broccoli, and carrots into characters that delighted everyone.

Cook Norm Lepitre with specially made creation for a delighted guest

"Eventually," says Lepitre, "we would take the theme of the week and incorporate it into the smorg decorations. For example, during Music Week I would carve instruments. The kitchen staff all had skills to make the smorg something special."

Winter Session students who helped to cook their own meals back in 1947 would perhaps marvel today at the new kitchen lights that use less power and cost less to buy. It's just one of many steps the centre has taken to make the kitchen more eco-friendly. Had anyone heard of trans fats 60 years ago? Today, the centre is trans-fat free. At a typical 2008 summer barbeque on the beach, there is far less plastic and more use of wooden cutlery and "already recycled" paper plates.

In the summer of 2007, the centre spent an average of $55,000 a month on groceries. Total for the year was $300,000.

The Sound of Music

Music has always infused Naramata Centre with joy and inspiration. Drums, guitars, pianos; voices – young and old; solo or en masse – have evoked the spirit that thrives at the centre. You hear it at community gatherings and celebrations, in worship, on the dance floor, in the chapel, at the beach, and under the trees.

Music has always been an important part of student life.

Within the first five years, Winter Session students had formed a choir and band. The choir sang at Naramata United Church on Sunday mornings, and occasionally at the United churches in Summerland and Penticton. The band played before vespers and at events in the local community.

The first Music Week, in 1962, was hosted by the Naramata Summer School of Music Arts Society. The society has since dissolved; nowadays, a Music Week Advisory Team works with the centre to create a Music Week summer program that people come back for year after year.

Music Week is always an opportunity for participants to discover talents and develop skills, and to share and celebrate choral music in community. Everyone is welcome, regardless of age or musical background. The centre has attracted excellent clinicians (professional choir leaders and choral teachers) whose skills are recognized both in Canada and the United States. Some people who have started singing here at an early age have gone on to have wonderful musical careers.

> *...everywhere I go, I hear music; you can hear it coming from all over the place, and it just melds together... it's exhilarating and calming at the same time.*
>
> ~ HEATHER RODGERS, MUSIC WEEK CO-ORDINATOR

The centre has long been supportive of new music, young musicians, and alternative musicians. Linnea Good, Jim Manley, Barb Myers, Bruce and Cheryl Harding, the Strathdees, and the band *Revolve*, among others, have found a home for their music there. "It's been a place where music supports the ["edgy"] theological stance of the centre," says Jim Strathdee.

Heather Rodgers has co-ordinated Music Week for nearly 20 years. "People have been coming for many years as families, and they love choral singing. It's not often that they find a place where they can experience a whole week of choral singing in a setting like this and be nourished in so many other ways. On Sunday night on the lawn, when you're waiting for opening celebration to start, there's a vibrant energy," says Rodgers.

In recent years, a young adult choir has been added, as well as a "green choir." "It's for folks who always thought they'd like to sing but didn't know music too well, or were intimidated by singing in a choir, to get them familiar singing with other people," says Rodgers.

With so much participant energy and time devoted to singing, the centre decided to create a more relaxed Music Week. "It's not quite so prescribed as it was," says Rodgers. "We try to cut back on the 'go-go-go' so people have more time with their families." In addition, the big push toward performing in a Friday evening concert has evolved, and the event is now more celebration than concert.

Some Naramata Centre Musical Heroes

Jean and Jim Strathdee

Jim and Jean Strathdee

Jim and Jean Strathdee have been singing and playing their way around the centre for nearly 40 years. In 1969, a friend who was teaching experiential worship at the centre asked Jim to come along and help with the music; Jim packed up his guitar and headed for Naramata. Subsequently, he was invited to be song leader at the B.C. Conference annual meeting in 1971. The centre then asked Jim and his wife, Jean, to perform concerts in congregations throughout Alberta and British Columbia. "We went through major cities as well as little places like Lillooet," recalls Jim. A centre staff member accompanied them and after the concert would stand up and talk passionately about the centre. The concerts, billed as *An Evening with Jim and Jean*, continued through the 1990s. Since then, the Strathdees have returned to the centre on a regular basis as music resource people. They also bring with them their experience in international volunteer work.

Says Jim, "Naramata really launched us in Canada. When the World Council of Churches came to Vancouver in 1983, we got to be part of it because we were so well loved at Naramata. Ten of our songs are in *Voices United*, the hymnal of the United Church of Canada."

Jean continues, "The centre has been very intentional about children and the inclusion of young people in all aspects whether it be planning or participation, and you see a lot of people come through here who have worked very strongly in the area of children's music. The centre has strongly influenced the United Church to be intentional about the inclusion of young adults, not only in music but in all areas of the church."

For the Strathdees, the use of music in the context of worship at the centre is particularly important. As summer music resource people, they plan the music to bring out the theme of the week and the theme of the summer. Says Jim,

> For example, for a summer theme *Rooted in Creation* and a week theme *Creatures of Sea and Sky*, we would think about songs that would relate to creation and spirituality. ... All of the creation needs to be seen as sacred for its own self and not as a commodity. How do you look at a forest? Some people see lumber; others see an eco-system. We bring to that context our own work, which has a variety of thematic streams: social justice, ecology, issues of poverty, and inclusion. That's probably one of the reasons that we've been invited back; they [our themes] are a good match to the themes that folks here care about.

Jim Manley

Jim Manley

Leading music for a week during the summer of 1980 was California minister Jim Manley's first introduction to the centre, and it marked the beginning of a relationship that continues to this day. While his wife, Judy, taught fabric art classes, Jim led music each evening, helped plan the Wednesday worship, and performed in a concert/singalong mid-week.

"I spent each morning with kids in a cluster on the lawn outside McLaren Hall, and taught songwriting classes to adults as well. The centre was already alive with environmental, peace, and justice concerns, so we felt very much at home with our art and music," says Manley.

He returned to the centre many times to lead music. Back home, he found himself writing songs with the centre in mind. "An inspiring two decades of experience," he says.

His memories include collaborating with Tim Scorer and the Wednesday worship planning team to create a service that "none of us could have imagined beforehand," and working with youth staff to create an all-female version of *The Prodigal Daughter* that left everyone in "tears and great laughter."

"We've never found a conference centre like Naramata in the [United] States, and frankly, there has been more than one camp or conference director who grew a bit tired of hearing about how things were done in the Okanagan," says Manley.

Linnea Good

Singer-songwriter Linnea Good has been a summer week music leader every year since 1986. She sees each new group as a single entity and pastors to it in that way. Good explains:

Linnea Good and partner David Jonsson

> Some weeks that "being" arrives worn, disheartened, and out of focus, seeking no more than rest. Other weeks it brings energy that is high, restless, or joyful. I have learned to ride the current of the group's own energy and help steer it toward an expression of the collective soul.
>
> In fact, this is where I have learned the most about how music can enhance the life of a community by drawing people into new ways of seeing God, articulating the kind of community we want to live in, giving flight to the cramped wings of our spirits, and, best of all, proving that faith can have a beat.

It was at Naramata Centre that I heard Sue Laverty ex-hort, "Use the scripture! Tell the stories of our faith!" At the microphone, Allison Rennie showed me that it was possible to stand silently in front of a large audience for full sec-onds, waiting confidently for the next right words to come. Jim and Jean Strathdee were the first to teach me that the words "God" and "justice" fell naturally together in song.

The toddlers who once sat next to Good on the piano bench have blossomed into today's music resource leaders. Parents confide that Naramata Centre is the only place where their teens will "put up" with Christian music. And much to Good's delight, children of all ages have entered the circle singing without reserve, "I am amazing! I am filled with power! And God loves me like crazy!"

Naramata

We come together in a special place
loving strangers and friends to embrace,
with helping hand and smiling face,
the family of God creating

We come to learn, we come to play,
quiet walks to begin the day,
to hear God's challenge
and learn to pray,
life's fullness celebrating

Naramata, smile of the sun,
God's healing gifts for everyone.
Naramata, our spirits renew,
may God always smile on you.[5]

~ *JIM STRATHDEE*

Congratulations, Naramata Centre!

🍇 Showing the world how to create multi-generational community where people of all ages are able to learn, worship, create, and lead together

🍇 Building and caring for a facility that is worthy to occupy one of the sacred sites in the Okanagan Valley

🍇 Becoming one of the important centres of leadership development in British Columbia and Alberta – in the church and in society at large

🍇 Developing relationships of hospitality and support with numerous organizations which have come to see the centre as their place for learning and community

🍇 Offering people a place of respectful and inclusive spirituality while still being clear about an identity within the tradition of the United Church

🍇 Existing and flourishing within the heart of a village and discovering a mutually beneficial relationship with the citizens of that surrounding community

🍇 Working at the cutting edge of education, bringing in outstanding teachers and innovative models of learning in numerous areas of human concern

🍇 Walking the financial tightrope of balancing the books while paying fair wages and maintaining a diverse 23-acre facility

🍇 Integrating the arts into the program life and learning environment of the centre

🍇 Challenging Christians in general and the United Church specifically to act for justice, live with diversity, and be the change they wish to see in the world

~ Tim Scorer

the centre in community

The centre recognizes that it must honour its position as an institution and one of the largest businesses in the community by paying attention to its relationships and being accountable to its neighbours. The pockets of hostility and mistrust have disappeared, so it would seem, through an emphasis on relationships.

Thanks to the perseverance and goodwill of many individuals and groups, the centre and the village of Naramata enjoy a harmonious relationship.

It wasn't always so.

"...People were not supportive of the centre. As teenagers we didn't want the centre here. None of us belonged to any church. We were pretty awful," says Berte Berry (nee Salting), who was born in Naramata in 1932.

Stu Berry arrived in Naramata in 1954 from Victoria, and got to know the co-founders, Bob and Alleen McLaren. "When I got here I was aware of this feeling. Bob was a developer, determined to make the centre go. He wasn't shy about asking for donations...In the beginning, there was a fair bit of support for the centre, but Bob's requests kept coming and that may have turned people off."

Some people were happy, such as the general store and coffee shop owners. In the very early days, local farmers and orchardists sold their produce at the centre; later, with many more visitors to feed, the centre turned to distant wholesalers for supplies.

"In its first couple of decades, the centre built up a lot of bad karma. It behaved imperiously and disrespectfully toward its community. It's not an unusual thing where you have an institution and a village," says former director Derek Evans. "...People were irritated for various reasons," he says, and cites one example of children unexpectedly discovering that their parents' house had been willed to Naramata Centre instead of to them.

Former Naramata Centre teacher and administrator Bill Adamson, who lived on centre property from 1964 to 1967, describes the relationship as "rather wary." "The village residents were not very happy with the large institution and its many visitors in the middle of their town! There were concerns about the water supply, the plumbing, the sewage field west of Columbia Hall, and possible pollution of the little creek that ran alongside the centre's property."

Darryl Auten, a former program staff member who lived both in the
village and at the centre from 1968 to 1977, picks up the story.

I thought we worked really hard, and we had a lot of support from the community, but there were people who were
fairly hostile toward us. We tried to encourage participation
of the young people from the community in things we did
winter and summer. The pool room was available to them.
The community always used Columbia Hall as a community centre...but there was tension. It was that old Oxford/

Darryl and Jeryl Auten with family

Cambridge thing – town and gown – and there were times people were not happy with us.

I think for some it was the fact that their quiet village was being invaded by people from afar. At the beginning, a lot of the work done around the grounds was done by people hired from the immediate area... But some folks moved here in the hope of connecting with the centre and getting jobs, and they brought specific skills; there were some splits over that... There were still lots of people who were ardent supporters, and their kids worked here, and the adults were involved in everything.

We also proposed closing some roads, and frankly, I'm glad now it didn't happen. At the time... it seemed a good idea. At a meeting one night in the library, people were yelling obscenities through the window as we tried to make a presentation. It was embarrassing.

I served on the Naramata Chamber of Commerce for five years trying to help bridge the gap, and subsequent staff have also done that and have found ways to build bridges, bring people in, and provide services that the community really couldn't have had otherwise.

By the time Marion and Jack Best came to work at the centre in 1977, tensions weren't quite as bad, but there was still a feeling that the community and the centre were separate. Few villagers took part in programs at the centre. Director Ivan Cumming and Nina Cumming attended the community church, but few other staff could go because they worked on Sundays.

"I don't remember outright animosity, but more indifference, or suspicion, or wondering about what went on [at the centre]," recalls Marion Best.

One breakthrough came when the centre started hiring local young people. Previously, kitchen, housekeeping, and grounds staff came from all over British Columbia and Alberta. The local people fit in very well and were available to work year-round.

Villagers were also concerned that the centre would keep growing and take over the community, but the centre committed to no new development. "I think that the community has appreciated that," says Marion Best.

One of the least congenial relationships occurred over a cinder path. The path (now Ellis Avenue) went from McLaren Hall up to 4th Street with an orchard on either side. Marion Best recalls the story.

> Even after the Maple Court units were built [in 1979], the hope was that it would remain a cinder path, and that they wouldn't put Ellis Avenue through, and that it would just be a walking path. Somebody in the community said, "They're [the centre] going to take over that property, and it's not theirs, and there's a road supposed to go there." I remember the day the bulldozers came and ploughed out all the trees and put Ellis through from 4th Street to 3rd Street."

Jack Best reflects that, "It divided the life of the centre in a way. People walk up and down and walk in the middle of the street in the summertime, and that annoys some local people."

Naramata Community Choir in concert at Columbia Hall, 1974

Columbia Hall became the place for community meetings, choir concerts at Christmas and old-age pensioners' dinners. But in 1977, a new facility was created in the village, with additions to the local elementary school. At the time, the centre advocated using the funds to make Columbia Hall a joint community place, instead of the school. The community was not in favour of that suggestion because the school district offered the community subsidized use of the new facilities for 20 years. When that arrangement ended in 2007 and the community had to begin paying to use the space, there was renewed interest in Columbia Hall. Today, the community has access to many centre facilities for a nominal charge.

The Naramata Community Choir performed its first concert at Columbia Hall in 1965 and continues to rehearse there twice a month. Since the mid-1970s, the choir has delighted audiences with its annual Christmas concerts at the centre.

The centre continues to contribute to the well-being of the community, notably during the disastrous firestorms that hit the South Okanagan in 2003. On August 16, forest fires quickly licked their way along the east side of the valley from Kelowna south to within a kilometre of rural Naramata. The situation was dire; the fire raged out of control. The village and surrounding areas were placed under an evacuation alert.

Grahame Baker, local fire chief and the centre's Facilities Supervisor, suggested to provincial emergency operations officials that they approach the centre for help. Staff quickly pulled together to provide accommodation and meals for up to 100 firefighters for six weeks. Local massage therapists and counsellors gathered at the centre and offered their services to the weary firefighters.

Thanks!

Aug. 27/03

For giving us a home away from home. Greatly appreciated. Tell the ladies who keep your location spic+span, excellent job + thanks for the big friendly smiles!

Assistant Chief Al Sutton
Captain Wayne Hamilton
Firefighters Jory Robinson
Roy Thomas
John Sheriff
Coquitlam Fire Rescue

Seniors Housing

More recently, in 2005, the centre sold a small parcel of property to the Naramata Seniors Housing Society, a group of volunteers who wanted to build seniors housing in the village. New housing units opened in 2007.

Although current executive director Andrew Church had heard stories of the centre's rocky relationship with the community, he didn't sense any animosity when he took over from Derek Evans in 2005. "I felt included as part of the centre, and I acted like I was part of the village and assumed that's what we were supposed to do...I'm involved in community life not because I should be but because...that's what I've always done," he says.

Church now chairs *Discover Naramata* (a group similar to a chamber of commerce), attends the Naramata Church, and takes part in the annual soapbox derby. "So in this village, the executive director is pretty visible. I feel like everyone knows me....I think I'm appearing to be like I want to be in the community and I want the centre to be a part of the community," he says.

In 2007, the centre provided some facilities at either no cost or break-even cost as a way to celebrate Naramata Village's 100th anniversary. For its contribution, the centre was later awarded an Outstanding Service Award by the Naramata Citizens Association. "It's a balance, so we're sensitive to the fact that we're non-profit," says Church. "For some groups, we have a community rate because they need to meet somewhere and they have it in their budget to pay."

"What I hear is that we are the community meeting spot for many groups. Some people describe us as the spiritual centre of the community. We didn't always used to be that," concludes Church.

In 2007, Naramata Centre received the Hospitality/Tourism Business Award sponsored by the Penticton and Wine Country Chamber of Commerce.

In 2008, Naramata Centre was publicly recognized by the Naramata Community Fund Society and the Naramata Market for its continuing support of both organizations.

Certificate of Appreciation

NARAMATA CENTRE

The Story of Naramata
Robinson's Rainbow
On to Naramata
April 6-7, 2007
Columbia Hall
Naramata Centre

This is to acknowledge your valuable assistance in the presentation of *Robinson's Rainbow---On to Naramata*. Your generous contribution has helped Naramata residents appreciate their heritage and celebrate the Centennial Year, 2007.

Naramata
1907   2007
Centennial
BRITISH COLUMBIA

Jane Shaak, Chair
Naramata Centennial Celebrations Committee
April 8, 2007

I remember the vivid stars when I arrived on a clear January night in 2008. I had never been to Naramata Centre before and didn't know what to expect, but I hoped that my three-and-a-half-month stay would be a time of challenge and change.

A line from a blessing by John O'Donohue says, "May you succumb to the danger of growth."[1]...In my experience at Winter Session, the danger of growth included being open and trusting the centre community. I felt blessed and grateful to accompany and be accompanied by others in learning and growing.

Winter in Naramata is sparse and beautiful. The vibrant blue of the sky contrasts with the warm yellows of the land; rocks and bare willow trees stand out of the landscape; there is quiet. Held by the simplicity of these surroundings, I felt free to break open and experience everything deeply. There was an abundance of ideas and emotions and I gained unexpected insights about the value of connection and the importance of combining creativity and spirituality. I loved the simple worship times, the long walks, and holding silence as a community. My time there felt like intentional living.

As I reflect on this experience, I realize that I continue to challenge myself to make lively decisions as I imagine new possibilities for the future.

BRYNA ANDRESSEN WAS A PARTICIPANT IN NARAMATA CENTRE'S 2008 WINTER SESSION, AND LIVES IN EDMONTON, ALBERTA.

governance

*What are the things we need to be
doing here to be relevant?*

~ ANDREW CHURCH, EXECUTIVE DIRECTOR

The centre is officially registered in the province of British Columbia as the Naramata Centre Society, and is a registered charity with the Canada Revenue Agency. It reports to the British Columbia Conference of the United Church of Canada. In 2008, there were about 500 Society members made of up of the board members; honorary members; Presbytery representatives from Alberta and British Columbia; congregational representatives from Alberta and British Columbia; and other interested individuals.

In 1967, the board decided that for legal purposes the name Christian Leadership Training School would be retained, but for common usage to adopt the name Naramata Centre for Continuing Education, United Church of Canada would be adopted.

There are 15 members on the centre's board of directors, including people from British Columbia Conference and Alberta and Northwest Conference. The constitution requires that two board members be under the age of 30.

There is an open invitation to anyone in the society to apply to be on the board. A nominating committee reviews the applications and presents those selected to the society's membership at its annual general meeting. As part of the review process, the committee assesses the current knowledge and skill set of the board and tailors recruitment to fill the skill gaps. Society members can also nominate people from the floor at the annual general meeting. Board members serve a three-year term, with the possibility of renewal for up to three years.

The inadequacy of road directions to the School was mentioned. It was agreed to stress the need of signs at the Penticton turn, in Naramata village itself, the turnoff to the School and such directions at the School itself that would prevent visitors arriving at the kitchen door.

(From the 1952 board minutes)

The original constitution of the Christian Leadership Training School of the United Church of Canada specified that the school have a board of 15 directors appointed by the Conference of B.C. of the United Church of Canada, and that the Conference invite executives of the Alberta, Saskatchewan and Manitoba conferences to submit one nomination each. Board members had a three-year term, and could be reappointed for two more terms. The chair and vice-chair were elected by the board.

The board was responsible for the general policy of the school and reported annually to the B.C. Conference, other interested Conferences, and to the board of Christian Education of the United Church of Canada (prior to 1972).

The board also appointed a Board of Trustees, Board of Managers, and the Principal. The five-member board of trustees was to hold all property in trust for the B.C. Conference and to manage the school's capital assets. The seven-member board of management was responsible for the day-to-day operations.

In the early 1950s, the board was expanded to include representatives from Presbyteries in British Columbia and Alberta. Over the long term, the up-to-30 member board proved unwieldy. In 1994, membership was reduced to 15, enabling it to deal with issues in more depth. The smaller board was better informed, and maintaining confidentially was easier. At the same time, the board wanted to move to a model where the authority of the board is vested in an executive director responsible for the day-to-day management of the centre and staff.

The board ultimately adopted a Policy Governance model[1]. One of the components of that model is a focused collaboration between the executive director and the board as partners in an exercise of leadership. It emphasizes measurable results and accountability.

The centre unveiled a new logo in 1978. It was designed by Willis Wheatley of Toronto, who said it denoted action and proclaims good news. In 1993 it was replaced by the current logo featuring two dancing figures, created by Vancouver artist Tiffanee Scorer.

Under the model, the board sets the mission, vision, and theological statements, along with the long-term goals and objectives for the organization. The executive director is the board's only employee, and along with a team, builds the strategies to achieve the board's plans.

Naramata Centre Board 2008
l to r: Wade Lifton, Pam Rinehart, Ron Spice, Wilma Geisbrecht, Alan Ford,
Barbara Gregg, Jim Simpson, Judy Hutchinson, Doug Woollard, Jenn Chocholacek,
Rosemary Best. Missing: John Burton, Michael Loewen

Three principals 1971

Reflections from Doug Woollard
Board Chair, 2008

Doug Woollard

Probably the most significant leadership shift has been the move from leadership by clergy to lay leadership. The knowledge and skills required to run the centre have led successive boards to hire executive directors who are not clergy. The centre has gradually shifted to serve a broader base than the United Church. The need to survive financially has forced a secular business response to maintain the facility. The leadership team must reflect this reality. So current leadership has more focus on running the business side than in the past.

> The centre receives operating revenue from programs and conferences, and non-operating revenue from the Vancouver Foundation, the Mustard Seed Bookstore, program grants, individual donations, and special fundraising.

The current challenge for the centre is to maintain the successful summer programming while expanding offerings consistent with the centre's mission in the spring and fall while maintaining the revenue currently generated by secular conferences. The second challenge is to raise the capital to rejuvenate the centre's physical capacity and implement a building improvement plan so the centre's buildings and infrastructure meet the needs of coming generations.

The Tennant Endowment Fund was established by Vernon residents Anna E. and Percival S. Tennant in 1963 with monies willed to the centre from the operations and subsequent sale of their gravel pit. As of December 2008, the fund was valued at about $818,500. A portion of the income from the fund is paid annually to the centre to offset operational expenses and capital programs.

Reflections from Andrew Church
Executive Director, 2008

People are really interested and passionate about what happens here. A lot of those folks are not members of the Society according to the bylaw – they don't vote – but they have this sense of ownership, and that's the group of people we want to stay in touch with. What are the things we need to be doing here to be relevant to them?

Andrew Church

The Board of Directors in 1957

Recruiting new students and promoting the Christian Leadership Training School were always concerns for boards in the early years. Board members continually urged ministers to be on the lookout for students and scholarship possibilities; to promote Friends of the School in their Presbyteries; to meet annually at the school; and to seek financial support for the school from key business people.

A list of questions regarding these topics was frequently posed to board members in advance of their annual meetings. This is the list from 1957.

- If one or two are an average number we could expect from each of our 445 pastoral charges each year, why are we not getting more of them?
- What are the real points of resistance with young people, young adults, and adults?
- Why do they fail to hear of the school?
- If they hear of the school, why don't they see it as meaningful themselves?
- What more could ministers, Sunday school staffs, mid-week leaders, and Christian Education Committee members do to clearly and challengingly present the opportunities for training at the school?
- What more could directors do?
- What could graduates be doing themselves and should churches use their services?

Wednesday Worship

A cathedral of light under the trees.

Walls are gone, what remains is a table of love.

Set with what we need: bread and wine: God's food.

Words of hope, burdens laid down, stories shared,
  deep songs sung.

A table set with acceptance, compassion, and hope.

Hearts breaking open all over the place, in soft light
  under trees.

The view of the lake, a blanket in the shade, a
  cathedral of light.

~ Doris Kizinna, 2007

chapter 8

over to you

My life-changing events have unfolded because of Naramata and for that I will keep this extraordinary place in my heart always.

~ Joan L. Becker

The words *Naramata Centre* often evoke powerful, positive, and fond memories in people who have experienced its magic. To help celebrate its history, the centre invited people to submit their special memories. Here is a selection.

>> *I remember back to 1958 when I was the lifeguard... Towards the end of each camp, I helped to organize a water sports event consisting of swimming races, diving competitions, and games. The most memorable game was one where a greased watermelon was thrown into deep water and the swimmer who got it onto the wharf got to keep the watermelon. This was for excellent swimmers only as it was quite rough!*

Since 1957, Naramata Centre has been an important part of my life and I hope it will continue to be there for future generations.

~ YVONNE FORBES (NEE CALLISTER)

>> *Sometime in the late 1990s, astronomers from all over the world gathered at the centre for a symposium. I was making my late-night rounds of the site when I heard a ruckus on the beach and ran down to see what was going on. A group of very excited astronomers was gathered on the dock, enthralled at witnessing a rare display of the northern lights. I saw a woman crying, and asked if I could help. "I've been an astronomer for 22 years," she replied, overcome with emotion. "I'm from Belgium, and I've never seen the northern lights." Then the group members ran to wake up others and share the joyous experience.*

~ DANNY MADIGAN, FORMER STAFF

>> To me, Naramata is LIFE
CHANGING – literally!

I first came to Naramata in
the summer of 2002. For over
20 years I had worked for the
National Broadcasting Company
(NBC) in Burbank, California.
My job was demanding, both of
my time and my spirit. I didn't
realize how much so until those
two weeks in Naramata.

Beyond the beauty of the
physical setting, Naramata has
its own spirit. Welcoming staff,
unique learning experiences,
and opportunities to cleanse
one's soul are just small parts
of the whole atmosphere. It was
easy to begin breaking down
walls that I had built around
myself for years. While talking
one night in the Maple Court
common area with my partner,
Amir Hussain, and Jim and Jean
Strathdee, I had an epiphany.
It became obvious to me that I
wanted to spend my life making a positive difference in the
world and that my current work
situation could not support
that dream. Amazing how clear
things can become when you are
in the Naramata "zone"!

Energized by my awakening,
and supported by my partner, I
left my job at NBC, returned to
university life, and received my
elementary teaching credential.
Now, I am greeted daily with
hugs and smiles from my students. We spend our time learning not only language arts and
mathematics but also music, art,
fairness, respect, and equality.
My hope is that my students are
learning as much about living
peacefully in this world as they
are about facts and information.

I remain grateful to Amir for
introducing me to Naramata
and for the support I have received from the many wonderful
friends we have made there.

~ JOAN L. BECKER

>> *The day I was to begin work at Naramata Centre, my car wouldn't start. So I had to phone and say what happened. The centre sent someone to pick me up. He was dressed in flowing robes and had a long beard. My kids, who were five and six at the time, were waiting for the school bus. They ran back to the house and said, "Dad, Jesus just came and picked up Mom for work."*

~ *Judy (Formo) Bateman*

>> *As a B.C. Conference staff member, I happened to be travelling near Naramata one day, and dropped into the centre for lunch. The dining room was packed, but I found a table and sat down in the only empty chair. I soon found out that everyone around the table was a First Nations chief. I was welcomed with warm smiles...When I asked what the conference was about, there was absolute silence. At last the man on my left, at the head of the table, responded, "LEADERSHIP – big subject, big as the world." Again silence. It was then I recognized the speaker as Chief Dan George![1] Conversation gradually resumed around the table and I chatted with the chief on my right, all the while uncomfortably aware that I was seated at the right hand of the honourable chief, in the chair that no one else felt worthy to occupy.*

~ *Jessie MacLeod*

>> *The first time I went to Naramata Centre my mom went for a course, and we shared a cabin with another lady and her family. The dads stayed home. I was probably six or seven. I remember having so much fun in the vacation school, playing on the grounds. We had one of those duplex cabins with a breezeway down the centre, and the fridge outside in the breezeway. That was the first time I had ever seen a fridge outside before – an unusual sight for a city kid! It was the first time I had ever slept in a bunk bed, too. They had these old army bunks with the metal frames...*

As I grew older, we went back to the centre many times, camping instead of "cabining." We roamed "wild and free" with the kids we made friends with. The sense of freedom was heady. We walked everywhere; going into the town for ice cream was a favourite activity.

I went to a spring session for teens. We spent a week, playing, laughing, and learning. I met a well-known football player who tried to teach us how to play a form of football called "razzle dazzle." I remember thinking that it was well named. My brain was razzled, if not dazzled. I later learned that he left football and became a United Church minister – cool!

I was a member of the summer staff in 1975 and I grew up a lot that summer. It was my first summer away from home, and although I did struggle with homesickness, I had a great time. Again, I experienced previously unknown freedoms there. It was a safe place to spread my wings...

As I look back, I realize my time as a kid at Naramata Centre opened lots of doors for me. Thanks, Naramata Centre. You taught me that I can try almost anything, and have a great time doing it!

~ LORRAINE WILSON (NEE ELLIOTT)

>> *Naramata baseball was a community game played on the McLaren Hall lawn. I believe it was invented by Bob McLaren himself... It was similar to regular baseball but involved a bigger ball, like a soccer or volleyball. Teams were huge and included people of all ages. The team up for kicking all stood along the south side of the lawn and the other team spread out. A pitcher would roll the ball to the kicker, who would kick the ball and run as fast as possible across the field. He or she was safe if they reached the line on the north side of the field by the creek before being hit by the ball thrown by the other team, in which case they were out. There they could rest until they tried to run back across the field to touch home base. Three outs and the teams traded places. It was a terrific game which involved the whole community, either playing or watching.*

~ KERRY ELLISON

appendix a

The United Church of Canada

The United Church of Canada is the largest Protestant denomination in Canada. It ministers to close to nearly three million people in 3,405 congregations across the country. Its rich history is closely entwined with the development of Canada itself.

The United Church was inaugurated on June 10, 1925, in Toronto, Ontario, when the Methodist Church, Canada; the Congregational Union of Canada; and 70 percent of the Presbyterian Church in Canada entered into an organic union.

As of December 31, 2006, the United Church was organized into 13 regional Conferences, 91 district Presbyteries, 2,269 local pastoral charges, and 3,405 individual congregations. Naramata Centre is one of four education centres established across Canada by the United Church: Calling Lakes Centre (Fort Qu'Appelle, Saskatchewan); Five Oaks Centre (Paris, Ontario); and Tatamagouche Centre (Tatagamouche, Nova Scotia). For more information on the centres and the United Church of Canada, contact:

The United Church of Canada
3250 Bloor St. West, Suite 300
Toronto, ON M8X 2Y4 Canada
Toll-free: 1-800-268-3781
Fax: 416-231-3103
Website: www.united-church.ca

A New Creed

We are not alone,
   we live in God's world.

We believe in God:
   who has created and is creating,
     who has come in Jesus,
     the Word made flesh,
   to reconcile and make new,
   who works in us and others
     by the Spirit.

We trust in God.

We are called to be the Church:
   to celebrate God's presence,
   to live with respect in Creation,
   to love and serve others,
   to seek justice and resist evil,
   to proclaim Jesus, crucified and risen,
     our judge and our hope.
In life, in death, in life beyond death,

   God is with us.

We are not alone.

   Thanks be to God.

A New Creed by The United Church of Canada, General Council, 1968, alt. from
Voices United: A Hymn and Worship Book, The United Church
Publishing House, 2007, p. 918. Used with permission.

Making Room for Women at the Archives

Making Room for Women AT THE ARCHIVES

The United Church of Canada
L'Église Unie du Canada

*M*aking Room for Women, a project of the Archives of the United Church of Canada, is a coordinated effort to identify and preserve the personal papers of women in The United Church of Canada and the records of organizations in which they have participated.

A key period of women's work, struggle, and leadership in the United Church coincided with the popularization of feminism in the wider culture 50 years ago. Organizations created during this time by women in both the United Church and the ecumenical church, such as the *Movement for Christian Feminism*, the *Ecumenical Decade of Churches in Solidarity with Women*, and the *Centre for Christian Studies*, are attracting scholarly interest.

As the leaders from this period are aging, now is the time to ensure that the experiences of its participants are collected for the archives.

If you come across any records (in any language) that tell a valuable story from this period, please get in touch with Making Room for Women (contacts below). Records of potential historical value include diaries and journals, correspondence, memoirs, scrapbooks, written-out sermons, addresses, articles, personal registers, datebooks, photographs, memorabilia, and audio/visual records.

Information: www.united-church.ca/archives/on/women/
E-mail: archives@united-church.ca
Tel: 416-231-7680, ext. 3123

appendix b

Naramata Centre Mission, Vision, and Theology Statements

Our Mission[1]

To be a place of learning, spiritual nurture, and renewal.

Our Vision

People are inspired to make a difference in the world.

Theology Statement[2]

We believe in God, who has created and is creating,
Who calls us into respectful relationship with all of Creation.

God's love has been shown to us in Jesus, through his life and teaching,
and through his prophetic practice of healing, hospitality, and radical
inclusion.

We believe this way of unconditional love is open to all people,
...those who are trusting, doubting, seeking, and knowing.
God is never separate from us.

Our Christian story gives us language and metaphor to share our stories,
and is one path to deeper relationship with ourselves, one another,
and God.

The Spirit is active in the world, embodied in us,
moving us into a life of bold love,
seeking justice and acting with compassion.

Rooted in gratitude and wonder,
experiencing God's unending grace and Holy mystery,
we listen for and live out God's call for the world.

Sample Summer Programs: 1964, 1978, 1995, and 2009

1964

program	leader
Youth Conclave & HI-C Counsellor Training	W. T. Briggs, Ivan Cumming
Sunday School Teachers and Mid-Week Leaders/Family Life Camp	Franck Patterson
Sunday School Teachers and Mid-Week Leaders	Clyde Woollard
Observation Practise School	Leader from Toronto United Church House
School of Religion and Life	Lona Fowler
School of Church Music	Frank Godley, Bob Wallace
Laymen in the Church	Bill Adamson
Family Life Camp	no leader listed

1978

program	leader
theme: *Participation Alive*	
Bible Study and the Congregation	Helen Stover Hunt
Telling My Story – Sharing My Faith	Jack and Marion Best
Learning with Adults	Nina and Ivan Cumming
Learning with Youth	Mardi Tindall
Learning with Children	Anne Searcy
Music in the Congregation	Don and Marg Waldon
Spiritual Re-Awakening	Gayda Errett
Audio/Visual Skillshop	Rod Booth
theme: *My Journey and Christian Community*	
My Journey and Christian Community	Ken Powers, Ivan Cumming
theme: *Growth Points*	
Coping with Stress	Art Chapple
Being Single	Elaine Peacock
Creative Divorce	John Stewart
Marriage Enrichment I	Ed and Mary Ette Branch

1978	
program	**leader**
Marriage Enrichment II	Jim and Lillian Ellis
Parenting	Pat and Glen Baker
Body and Soul	Roy Wood
Faith and Imagination – Creative Writing	Will Morrison
Beginners Pottery	Carolyn Wallace
theme: Futures, Possible, Probably, Preferable	
Theology and the Faith Ahead	Richard H. Overman
French/English Relations – Future of Canada	Guy DesChamps
Social-Political Economic Futures	John Foster
Ethics and Genetic Engineering	Bruce Hatfield
Futures in Health Services	Frank McNair
Futures in Education	Larry Blake
Green Earth	Norm and Joyce Scott
theme: Summer School of Music Arts	
Summer School of Music Arts	Alice Parker, John Yarrington, Betty Ann Ramseth, Norman Hunter
theme: Search for Justice in a Hurting World	
Liberation Bible Study	Jim Lindenberger
The Church and Criminal Justice – "Alternatives"	Dave McCord
Poverty: The Flip Side of Canada's Wealth	Bob Lindsey
Men/Women and Liberation	Adrienne Kemble
Hope in the Midst of Darkness	Wes Maultsaid
Being Christian in a Violent World	George Hermanson
English Smocking	Mary Gagnon
Wood Sculpture	George Gabb
theme: Celebrating Creativity Arts & Faith	
Pottery – Wheel	Bruce Lussier
Pottery – Hand-building	Rod and Joan Butler
Wood Sculpture	George Gabb
Oil Painting	Allan Jones
Off-Loom Weaving	Merna Beeny
Photography: Inner Vision/Outer Vision	Jim Cluett

1978	
program	**leader**
Sketching	Dennis Fjestad
Birdwatching	Ray Cromie
Hawaiian Quilting and Appliqué	Nevione Crawford
theme: Youth Conclave	
Youth Conclave	Bruce Griffin and Catherine Ross

1995	
program	**leader**
theme: Getting It All Together	
Brass Tacks and Grass Roots	Don Milne, Peter Osborne
theme: Naramata Summer School of Music Arts	
Naramata Summer School of Music Arts	Linda Spevacek, Brian Farrell, Catherine Glaser-Climie
theme: Outside the Lines	
New Hope for Relationship	Alex and Joy Lawson
Birdwatching	Ray Cromie
Writing (Right) Between the Lines	Hazel Smith
Seasons of the Feminine Divine	Kay Schmitt
Flying without Wings	Harold Naka
Cultivating Children's Values	Elaine Jaltema
The Enneagram – An Ancient Tool for Spiritual Transformation	Dawn Kilarski
Nourishing the Roots of Men's Spiritual Lives	Tom Hunter
Dream Circle	Stan McKay
Senior Teens	Debbie Hemmens
theme: Getting Focused	
Healthy Sexuality for Families	Meg Hickling
Faith: Framed and Focused	Jack Jervis and Lori Stewart-Jervis
What Did Jesus Really Say?	Bruce Miller
Soul Work and Playtime	Garnet Thomas
Seeing into Nature: A Photography Workshop	Adele Curtis
To Gladden the Human Heart – The Theology and Art of Wine	Ed Searcy

1995	
program	**leader**
Pottery	Pat Krug
Rain to the Desert: Healing WomanSpirit through the Arts	dori petty
Life to the Children!	Omega Bula
Senior Teens	Jennifer and Ian Cunnings
theme: Give Us This Day	
The Hand of Charlemagne – Lettering and Calligraphy, Gilding and Illumination	Bev Bunker
Clearing in the Morning	Carolyn McDade
The Gourmet Camper	Chris Crosthwaite
Making the Ordinary Holy	Leah Green
Mary, Martha and More; Biblical Women in Focus	Caryn Douglas
Christianity at the Edge	Ed Searcy
Pottery	Pat Krug
Writing Down the Day	Rebecca Luce-Kapler
Heart and Soul	Jo-Ann Stansfield
Senior Teens	Doris Kizinna
theme: Homeward Bound	
Parenting	Bev and Andrew Church
Let the Song Speak	Barry Luft
Passive Solar Water Heater: A Hands-on Construction Workshop	Anthony Stoppiello
Drawing the Artist Within: Creative Encounters	Valerie Pugh
At Home to the World	Jim and Deborah Marshall
Voicing Our Unbelief	David Ewart
Dancing Our Journey	Celeste Schroeder
Pottery	Yvonne Jordan
Home...Work...and Being	Ivan Cumming
Senior Teens	Susan Fitch
theme: Gifts and Promises	
Leaps of Faith	Keri Wehlander
Healing Touch	Shelley Graham

1995	
program	**leader**
Out of Zinn, God Shines Forth	Joan Poulin
Chaos to Consensus: Discovering Skills for Conflict within Community	Gordon Sloan
You Gotta Have Heart	Laurie Hardingham, Helen Coskuner
Living between Survival and Hope	Valerie Ross
Pottery	Yvonne Jordan
Celebrating God in the Wilderness	Brian and Kathryn Christian
The Spirituality of Children	Geoffrey Wilfong-Pritchard
Senior Teens	Cheryl Perry
theme: Rules and Opportunities	
Line Dancing	Barb and Gary Dean
Express Yourself: African Drumming	Dido
Hiking and Biking	Don and Jay Milne
Yes I Can; Draw and Paint	Margaret Vouladakis
Catching Creativity	dori petty and summer staff
Introductory Canoeing	Dierdre and Doug Goodwin
Something from the Earth	Peggy Evans, David Galeski
Wooden Toy Making	Bill Birse
You Can Stencil	Joan MacDonald
Teddy Bear Magic	Joan Chambers
Magic, Clowning, and Storytelling	The Jaltema Family
Wonder Play in God's Creation	Brian and Kathryn Christian
Discovery through Movement	Yarrow Sheehan
Experience Integral Yoga	Mugs Mahler

Summer Programs, 2009

Decisions on what summer programs to offer continue to reflect the theme and purpose of the centre. In 2009, the theme is "Common Table, Common Wealth."

"...Naramata Centre invites each of us to remember the abundance that is ours at the common table. In these times of shifts in power and all kinds of uncertainty, amidst change and loss, we each have many blessings if only we count the simple things – a place to live, food for the day, a friend, the ability to offer our unique gifts to the world. How do we find the discipline to honour the simple rhythm of gathering at the table with others? How do we make space and time in our daily lives for sharing stories of change, justice and hope? This summer, week by week, we will gather as a table to take time, be with one another, and practice living in Christian community."

2009	
program	**leader**
theme: What's for Dinner? (Intergenerational)	
Pottery	Carol Marshall and Bryna Andressen
Whole Family Cooking	Norm Lepitre
Sing! Sing! Sing!	Bonnie Ferguson
Fed by Our Stories	David Roche and Marlena Blavin
A Taste of the Arts – Sharing Your Creative Spirit	Barbara Karmazyn
Cartooning – Your Life as a Comic Book!	Brian Tate
Spirit Drum	Lyle Povah
Stained Glass Mosaics	Joan Chambers
Introduction to Papermaking	Sheri Silcox
Collective Creation in New Media	Barbara Anderson and Tom Anderson
Round and Round the Table: Labyrinth and Mandala	Glynis Wilson Boultbee
Social Dancing	Barb Child
Hiking – Loving the Land	Julia Lynx and Bonnie Hamilton
Yoga for All Ages	Mugs McConnell
Games for All Ages	summer staff

2009	
program	**leader**
theme: Who's Coming for Dinner?	
Pottery	Catherine Epps
I'm Coming to Dinner: Exploring Self-Image through Art Making	Susanna Ruebsaat
Meeting Your Neighbour	Karen Rolston and Parker Johnson
Encountering the Sacred Other in Scripture	Ross Smillie
Singing – Stand on the Rock and Shout with Joy	Linnea Good
Fabric Collage	Margie Davidson
Discovering the Stranger in Contemporary Cinema	Lori Stewart and Jack Jervis
Encountering Local Flora and Fauna	Dick Cannings and Margaret Holm
Soccer	Jim Cryder
theme: Time for dinner!	
Pottery	Catherine Epps and Pat Krug
Laugh Alive! – Creating Joy through Laughter Yoga	Hugh McCelland
Healing Pathway Phase 1	Catherine Awai and Ross White
Shabbat: Jewish Teachings on Simple Acts that Renew	Rabbi Laura Kaplan
Living Flowers – Introduction to Ikebana	Masako and Lynn Ryan
Threshold Choir – Singing with Care	Linda Allen
Preserving Our Food	Peggy Evans
Sacred Circle Dance	mihaela
Sea Kayaking	Peter Price and Lynne Whiskin
Introduction to Christian Spiritual Practices	Maya Landell
theme: Are We Going to Say Grace?	
Pottery	Angela Carlson
Interfaith Dialogue	Hillel Goelman, Amir Hussain, and Tim Scorer
Introduction to Massage	Sandy LeCour
Enneagram	Dawn Kilarski and Barry Vall
Dream Catchers	Wii Haughtkm Skiik
Printmaking	Julie Elliot
Digital Photography Level 2	Skai Fowler
Basket Making	Martha Cloudesley
Yoga for Grace	Wildflower
Rooted in Nature	Michael Barr and Laurie Moffitt Barr
Your Voice, Your Power	David Hatfield
theme: Bring It to the Table	
Pottery	Dennis Evans

2009	
program	**leader**
Jung's Typology: Bringing the Magnificent 16 to the Table	Danielle Poirier
Speaking Our Truth in a Diverse World	Brian Frank
Safe Haven for Questions	Nancy Talbot
Vibrant Oil Colours	Gail Thomas
Gospel Choir – Bring it! Sing it!	Louise Rose
The Universe through the Eyes of an Astronomer	Chris Purton
Road Biking – Finding Your Place in the Peloton of Life	Willi Fast
Tai Chi	Hajime Naka
Bring It On!	Diana Brecka
theme: Listen to This!	
Pottery	Darryl Auten
Grades 1-3 Choir and Program	Janet Rendell
Grades 4-6 Choir and Program	Janet Rendell
Grades 7-9 Youth Program	Bruce Cable
Grades 10-12 Youth Program	Bruce Cable
Young Adult Choir	Scott Leithead
Green Choir	Liz Paynter
Grand Choir	Laurier Fagnan
Pottery	Darryl Auten and Bryna Andressen
theme: *Setting the Table*	
Pottery	Darryl Auten and Bryna Andressen
Scrapbooking, Storytelling and the Spirit	Pamela Jeffery and Mary Nichol
Massage for All Ages	Brenda Wilkinson
Mission – Extending the Table	Michael Shewberg
Piggy Banks and Biggie Banks	Sheila Munroe and Gladys Fraser
Singing, Rhythm, and Body Percussion	Dawn Pemberton and Karla Mundy
Knitting for the Soul	Esther Kaiser
Felting Revival	Kerry Ellison
Drama-o-rama	Wade Lifton
Songwriting	Brendan Wanderer
Arts for the Table – Tie Dye and More	Tressa Brotsky
Tai Chi for All Ages	Hajime Naka
Games – Play, Explore, Run and Restore!	Cathy Cryder
Canoeing	Katy Cox and Elijah Brownlee
When You Walk from Here	Phil McIntyre-Paul
The Writing Table – Stories about Me	Anne Fleming

Spicy Squash Soup

This recipe is a Naramata "original," developed around 1994. Food Services Supervisor Colin Drought says this has been the most requested soup since then. It's delicious.
Thanks Colin!

Serves 30. You can cut the recipe in half or quarters. Freezes well.

Ingredients

2 tbsp	oil	1 tsp	ground pepper
3 cups	onions, chopped	½ tsp	lemon rind, grated
2	cloves garlic, minced	½ tsp	turmeric
1½ cups	celery, chopped	½ tsp	hot pepper flakes
½ cup	fresh ginger, minced	16 cups	squash, diced
½ cup	fresh cilantro, chopped	2 cups	tomatoes, diced (fresh or tinned)
4 tsp	coriander seeds	2	14-oz cans coconut milk
2 tsp	ground cumin	½ cup	fresh parsley or cilantro, chopped (to garnish)
1 tsp	salt		

Directions

Heat the oil in a large soup pot over medium heat and sauté onions, garlic, celery, ginger, and coriander seeds until onion is translucent but not browned. Make sure garlic and seeds do not burn. Add all the other ingredients except coconut milk and parsley. Cover and cook until squash is tender (add water as needed). Puree (use an immersion blender or a food processor) until smooth. Add the coconut milk 20 minutes before serving and reheat gently. Stir in the chopped parsley or cilantro just before serving or leave it out of the soup and sprinkle some on each serving.

Greening Naramata Centre 2008

Here are some things Naramata Centre is doing to practise environmental stewardship.

Reducing impact on the environment by

- printing on 100 percent post-consumer waste recycled paper
- reviewing wastewater management system and implementing upgrades
- planning for capital development with attention to reducing impact on the environment
- protecting Naramata Creek by continuing to work with the Naramata Environmental Action Team, Naramata Creek Committee, and the Naramata Conservation Society
- planning to enhance the riparian zone
- planting trees, removing invasive weeds on the clay bank

Reducing energy use by

- using compact fluorescent light bulbs wherever possible
- turning lights off when not in use
- upgrading to high efficiency fluorescents in classrooms
- investigating fuel efficient options for guest transportation and on-site vehicles
- replacing fridges with new energy smart models and recycling the old ones
- installing solar water heating in Columbia Hall

Reducing water use by

- changing bedding only at the end of each guest's stay (not daily)
- upgrading to low-flow showerheads and low-flush toilets
- converting water intensive gardens to xeriscape (low water use, low maintenance)
- using compost and woodchip mulch for water retention in gardens
- reducing irrigation

Reducing waste by

- recycling paper, plastics, metals, glass, batteries
- composting yard waste
- reusing paper whenever possible

Reducing vehicle impact by

- carpooling, ride-sharing; holding web-based meetings, using conference calls
- using energy efficient vehicles for transporting guests and working on-site

Naramata Centre Board Chairs

1947-51	Mortimer Lees		1978-81	Frank Williams
1951-56	Jack Robinson		1982-87	Frank McNair
1956	Jack Robinson/ D.H. Telfer		1988-91	Jack Shaver
			1992-96	Stan Walker
1957	Roy Johnson		1997-99	Catherine Awai
1958	Roy Johnson/ Russell Ross		1999-2001	Rita Cattell
			2002	Doug Goodwin
1959	D. H. Telfer		2003-04	Greg Bell
1960-68	Charles Burritt		2005-06	Jane Ritchie
1969-74	Jake Peters		2007-	Doug Woollard
1975-77	Gordon Sladen			

Note: Some dates overlap due to mid-year role changes

Principals and Executive Directors

1947-1964	Bob McLaren (Principal)
1965-1968	Franck Patterson (Principal)
1968-1981	Ivan Cumming (Director)
1981-1986	John Robertson (Director)
1987-1992	Staff Administration Team
1992-1994	Tim Scorer (Director)
1994-1999	Mary Robertson (Director)
2000-2004	Derek Evans (Executive director)
2005-	Andrew Church (Executive director)

Note: Some dates overlap due to mid-year role changes

The Team Model

The success of the centre has been in part due to the management team model that it operates under. It is important to recognize the hundreds of other men and women who worked together collaboratively and collegially in program and management teams and made important contributions to the successes and strengths of the centre. It is also important to recognize that the board and management positions in the lists were held mainly by men, and to honour the many women who have made and continue to make important contributions to the centre's health and leadership.

The management team, 2003.
back, l to r: Diane Ransom, Tim Scorer, Allison Rennie
front, l to r: Catherine Awai, Derek Evans

Honorary Members of the Naramata Centre Society, 2008

Darryl Auten, past program staff member

Jeryl Auten, friend, volunteer, and supporter

Catherine Awai, past board chair, past director of the Healing Pathway and past chair of the Chapel Committee

Jack Best, past program staff member

Marion Best, past program staff member; former Moderator of the United Church of Canada

*Ivan Cumming, past director of the centre, co-founder of Training Learning Consulting Associates

Nina Cumming, co-founder of Training Learning Consulting Associates

Jim Ellis, past member of the board of directors

Gilbert Giesbrecht, co-creator of the labyrinth

Wilma Giesbrecht, co-creator of the labyrinth, current member of the board of directors, member of the Healing Pathway advisory team

Rochelle Graham, founder of the Healing Pathway

*Sue Laverty, past program staff member

Alleen McLaren, co-founder

*Bob McLaren, co-founder, past principal

*Frank McNair, past board chair

*Phyllis Mattham, friend, volunteer, and supporter

John Robertson, past director of the centre, program staff member, and Trustee

Mary Robertson, past director of the centre and program staff member

Donna Scorer, established Children's House

Tim Scorer, past director of the centre and program staff member

Joyce Scott, attended for 35 years in a row

*Norm Scott, attended for 35 years in a row

George Searcy, past member of the board of directors

*Alice Stobie, long-time supporter, tutored First Nations in residence

*Roy Stobie, founding team member, past staff member

Jean Stobie, long-time supporter, past program staff member

Jim Strathdee, long-time music resource person

Jean Strathdee, long-time music resource person

Eric Tollefson, co-founder of Special Needs Program

Jean Tollefson, co-founder of Special Needs Program, past program committee member, and member of the board of directors

*Clyde Woollard, founding team member, past vice-principal

Dorothy Woollard, spouse of former staff member, volunteer, supporter

*deceased

appendix c

Thank you to the following sponsors for their financial contributions to help create this book:

Darryl and Jeryl Auten
Catherine Awai
BCGEU Component 12
Bruce & Brenda Bearisto
Jack & Marion Best
Rosemary Best & Jim Stephen
Brian Campbell
Pauline Carson
Andrew Church
Bev Church
Shirley Coolidge
Hans & Helen denBoer
Kerry Ellison & Kevin McLachlan
Barbara Gregg & Harry Steele
Marnie Harrison
Barbara Hatfield & Rob Coles
  & family
Kathleen & Bruce Hatfield
Amir Hussain & Joan Becker
Jean MacLeod
Lynn Maki

Barb McFadyen-Smuin &
  Ron Smuin
Christopher & Vicki McPhee
John & Donna McTaggart
Ruth McWhinnie
Marilyn Negropontes
Ron & Marjean Park
Allison Rennie & Diane Ransom
Mary & John Robertson
Robin & John Robertson
Louise Rose
Jim and Donna Simpson
Rae Slavens
Jeff Smuin
Lorraine Struyk
Bob & Marion Taylor
West Coast Family Support
  Institute
Nancy & Garnet Wolchok
Joyce Wright

Thank you to the following people who contributed to the making of this book.

Bill Adamson

Bryna Andressen

Darryl Auten

Catherine Awai

Grahame Baker

Judy Bateman (nee Formo)

Joan Becker

Berte Berry

Stu Berry

Gerry Bell

Bob Bell

Jack Best

Marion Best

Jack Booth

Peggy Booth

Graham Brownmiller

Isabel Chen

Andrew Church

Johnny Clermont

Sylvia Colclough (nee Cooke)

Nina Cumming

Colin Drought

Jody Dudley

Jim Ellis

Kerry Ellison

Derek Evans

Family Support Institute

Berta Fisher

Lawrie Fisher

Yvonne Forbes (nee Callister)

Julie Gerhardt

Gilbert Giesbrecht

Wilma Giesbrecht

David Giuliano

Linnea Good

Chris Grauer

Anita Greenaway (nee Stewart)

Barb Hatfield

Sue Hatfield

Ryan James

Doris Kizinna

Arlene Kropp

Norm Lepitre

Po-Yi Liu

Jean MacLeod

Jessie MacLeod

Mugs McConnell

Carol McGibney

Barb McFadyen-Smuin

Alleen McLaren

Ali Adams Nelner

Donna McTaggart

John McTaggart

Danny Madigan

Arnold Maki

Lynn Maki

Jim Manley

Sarah Morgan (nee Bartner)

John Moss
Bill Mussel
Marion Mussell
Elaine Peacock
Dave Perry
Diane Ransom
Allison Rennie
Betty Richards
John Robertson
Mary Robertson
Robin Robertson
Heather Rodgers
George Rodgers
Tim Scorer
Wii Haughtkm Skiik (Don M. McKay)

Linda Sherwood
Gabe Stickland
Bob Stobie
Jean Stobie
Jean Strathdee
Jim Strathdee
Bob Taylor
Marion Taylor
Susan Telfer
Jean Tollefson
Neil Trainer
Dirk van Battum
Terry Whyte
Lorraine Wilson (nee Elliott)
Doug Woollard

Thanks also to

Blair Galston, Conference Archivist, British Columbia Conference,
   United Church of Canada, The Bob Stewart Archives, Vancouver
The Hatfield family from Alberta
Barb McFadyen-Smuin, volunteer History Book Project co-ordinator,
   Naramata Centre
Bill and Jean Molyneux
Naramata Centre office staff
Peter Ord, Manager/Curator, Penticton Museum & Archives
Debra Potter, General Manager of Finance, Regional District of
   Okanagan-Similkameen
Reviewers: Bryna Andressen, Catherine Awai, Jack Best, Marion Best,
   Andrew Church, Wade Lifton, Allison Rennie, John Robertson,
   Mary Robertson, Mandy Wheelright
Diane Ransom, Naramata Centre management staff advisor to the
   History Book Project
Jane Ritchie
Ron Smuin
Jim Taggart
Nichole Vonk, General Council Archivist, United Church of Canada,
   Toronto

Sources
- Interviews by the author
- Board of directors minutes 1947 to 1948
- *Naramata*, by Dr. W. J. Rose, Christian Leadership Training School,
   1963
- Program brochures, yearbooks, and memorabilia
- Videos[1]
- Naramata Centre Master Site Plan October 19, 2007

endnotes

Chapter 1

1   The Board of Christian Education Field Secretaries were national staff responsible for leadership training and providing resources for clergy, church school, and mid-week group leaders (i.e., CGIT, Explorers, Tyros) in congregations.

2   Archival material from the 1940s relating to Naramata Centre's formation and early days features the roles and contributions of men more predominantly than women. Clearly the rise and acceptance of feminism in the years since then has resulted in a new societal perception of women's roles. In 2008, centre co-founder Alleen McLaren acknowledged several women for their support in establishing the Christian Leadership Training School, mentoring Bob McLaren and hosting him when he made visits to Vancouver, and donating goods. They are June Burritt, Bea Magar, Olive Sanford, Jennie Robinson, Ruth Simpson, Minnie Villet, and Agnes Williamson.

    The United Church of Canada has recognized that a key period of women's work, struggle, and leadership in the church coincided with the rise of feminism in the wider culture. Please see Appendix A for information on the project Making Room for Women at the Archives.

3   Possibly Naramata Nominating Committee

4   Heartwood, Growth from the Centre, (Naramata, Naramata Centre, 1987) p. 8 (Note: There was an editorial committee, but not one author. The committee was chaired by Marion Taylor.)

5   See more about the Naramata Centre labs on page 69.

Chapter 2

1   The courses for the first year included Introducing the Bible, Understanding Our Faith, The Christian Way, The Church through the Ages, The World Mission of Christianity, Home Missions, The Church and the Christian in Society, Principles of Learning and Teaching, The Sunday School, Public Speaking and Platform Presence, Church Music and Worship and Its Leadership in Church and Group.

2   A fag is a term for a British public school boy acting as a servant.

3   The Bell System of the Christian Leadership Training School (from *The Gateway*, a publication of the C.L.T.S. graduating class, 1952)

Chapter 3

1   *The Good News* (March 1979)
2   Ivan Cumming was the centre's Director from 1968 to 1981.
3   Some United Church congregations are designated as "affirming congregations," which means they have gone through a process to openly welcome gays, lesbians, bisexual, and transgendered people and their families.
4   Kerry Ellison's parents, Margaret and Bruce Ellison, attended their first summer program in 1956. Kerry has five siblings.
5   Also see Healing House page 131.
6   *The Observer*, Vol. 14, No. 10, April 1978, page 15.
7   dori petty uses lower case for her name

Chapter 4

1   Over the years, Naramata Centre expanded to its current size by acquiring nearby properties as they came available for purchase and as funds permitted.
2   Gloria Sawai, writer-in-residence 1982. Used by permission.

Chapter 5

1   dori petty uses all lower case when writing her name
2   Students completing the Healing Pathway curriculum are required to offer treatments in the Healing House as part of the Practicum A.
3   See Appendix B for a delicious soup recipe from the kitchen of Naramata Centre.
4   British term for piece of drudgery, a wearisome or unwelcome task
5   Words and music by Jim Strathdee. © 1987 by Desert Flower Music. Commissioned by the centre to help celebrate its 40th anniversary.

Chapter 6

1   John O'Donohoe, *Eternal Echoes* (New York, HarperCollins, 1999)

Chapter 7

1   Author John Carver is internationally known for his work in board leadership called the Policy Governance® model. He is the author or co-author of several books, including *John Carver on Board Leadership, Boards That Make a Difference: A New Design for Leadership in Nonprofit and Public Organizations.*

Chapter 8

1   Chief Dan George (1899–1981) was a chief of the Tsleil-Waututh Nation in North Vancouver, B.C. He was also an actor and author.

Appendix B

1   The mission and vision statements evolved out of a previous mission statement and were the result of board/management collaboration during a 2006 Strategic Planning event. The statements were approved by the board in April 2006.

2   A subcommittee of two board members and two managers formulated the theology statement, which was approved by the board in January 2008.

Appendix C

1   The author viewed three videos that were found in a box in the basement at the centre. All were undated. The first was labelled Naramata Winter Session (B.C. Conference Video Production). The second was labelled #2, 1-5 and was about Naramata Centre's 50th anniversary celebrations in 1997. The third was labelled Naramata and was hosted by J. Frank Willis. It was originally a film about the United Church's four retreat centres across Canada and looked like it had been produced in the 1950s. This may be the film referred to in the 1957 director's minutes: *Dr. Cooper informed us that Anson Moorehouse will produce a sound film, documentary in style, with the Christian Leadership Training Centres as subjects. This film, costing $10,000, will be ready in 1960.*

photo credits

p. 8   © Naramata Centre
p. 10   © Tim Yip photo
p. 12   © Wood Lake Publishing
p. 15   © ET2 Productions
p. 16   © The United Church of Canada
        Used with permission
p.22   © Naramata Centre
p. 24   © Penticton United Church
p. 27   © Sarah Morgan
p. 28   © The Bob Stewart Archives of the
        United Church of Canada, B.C.
        Conference
p. 31   © Alleen McLaren
p. 33   © Naramata Centre
p. 34   © Naramata Centre
p. 36   © Alleen McLaren
p. 37   © Naramata Centre
p. 40   © Naramata Centre
p. 42   © Naramata Centre
p. 44   © Lone Jones
p. 48   © Sarah Morgan
p. 49   © The Bob Stewart Archives of the
        United Church of Canada, B.C.
        Conference
p. 50   © The Bob Stewart Archives of the
        United Church of Canada, B.C.
        Conference
p. 53   © Bruce Hatfield
p. 54   © Naramata Centre
p. 57   © The Bob Stewart Archives of the
        United Church of Canada, B.C.
        Conference
p. 58   © Naramata Centre
p. 59   © The Bob Stewart Archives of the
        United Church of Canada, B.C.
        Conference
p. 63   © Chris Grauer
p. 64   © Naramata Centre
p. 66   © Naramata Centre
p. 74   © Bert Ellison
p. 75   © Naramata Centre
p. 76   © Bert Ellison
p. 77   © Bert Ellison

P. 78   © Bruce Hatfield
p. 79   top © Neil Trainer
        bottom © Naramata Centre
p. 83   © Naramata Centre
p. 86   © Naramata Centre
p. 88   © The Bob Stewart Archives of the
        United Church of Canada, B.C.
        Conference
p. 90   © Naramata Centre
p. 91   © dori petty
p. 92   © Naramata Centre
p. 93   © Naramata Centre
p. 94   © Naramata Centre
p. 96   © Naramata Centre
p. 98   © Stocks Camera
p. 99   © The Bob Stewart Archives of the
        United Church of Canada, B.C.
        Conference
p. 101 © Naramata Centre
p. 102 © Naramata Centre
p. 105 © Naramata Centre
p. 107 © Naramata Centre
p. 108 © Naramata Centre
p. 110 © Naramata Centre
p. 115 © Naramata Centre
p. 117 © Naramata Centre
p. 118 © Naramata Centre
p. 120 © Naramata Centre
p. 124 © Naramata Centre
p. 126 © Naramata Centre
p. 129 © Naramata Centre
p. 131 © Naramata Centre
p. 133 © Naramata Centre
p. 134 © Naramata Centre
p. 135 © Chris Grauer
p. 136 © Chris Grauer
p. 138 © Chris Grauer
p. 139 © Naramata Centre
p. 141 © Naramata Centre
p. 142 © Bruce Hatfield
p. 144 © Naramata Centre
p. 145 © Naramata Centre
p. 146 © Naramata Centre

MARY TRAINER has been writing about British Columbia people, places, history, and environment for nearly 40 years. Born and raised in Summerland, B.C., Mary is a graduate of British Columbia Institute of Technology and Simon Fraser University. In the 1970s, she was one of three publishers with Nunaga Press, which published 16 books on B.C. history and recreation. In 1973, she wrote A History of Policing in Burnaby, 1892-1950, and was commissioned to write Tales of a B.C. Trucker in 1985. In 2007, she co-authored the Canadian bestseller Slumach's Gold: In Search of a Legend with Brian Antonson and Rick Antonson.

Mary worked in corporate communications at Simon Fraser University and the Metro Vancouver Regional District for 30 years. She was the 2004 winner of the International Business Communicators Association Blue Wave Award of Excellence in Features and Editorial Writing.

A passionate cruciverbalist, Mary has created many acrostic puzzles (featuring Canadian clues) to challenge readers of the alumni journals of Simon Fraser University, the University of British Columbia, and the University of Manitoba; Books in Canada; The Vancouver Sun; and BC Bookworld. Mary has also written articles for numerous magazines, newspapers, trade, and alumni journals.

In addition to a love of B.C. history, Mary's interests include gardening, biking, writing, reading, volunteering, and listening to jazz. She lives in Summerland, B.C.